How to Analyze People

Successful Guide to Human Psychology, Body Language And How to Read People Instantly

2nd Edition

Fred Cremone

information is without contract or any type of guarantee assurance.

The trademarks that are used are without any consent, and the publication of the trademark is without permission or backing by the trademark owner. All trademarks and brands within this book are for clarifying purposes only and are the owned by the owners themselves, not affiliated with this document.

Table of Contents

Introduction   1

Chapter 1: Language- The Nonverbal Canvas   3

Chapter 2: The Cultural Dimensions of Body Language   10

Chapter 3: Haptics   14

Chapter 4: When is it Appropriate to Touch?   23

Chapter 5: Eye Contact   35

Chapter 6: Smiles and Laughter   38

Chapter 7: The Study of Proxemics   43

Chapter 8: Sitting Body Language   59

Chapter 9: The Use of Body Language   65

Chapter 10: Types of body language   73

    Parts of the body   73

    The intent of using the body language   76

Chapter 11: Message Clusters Delivered Through Body Language   78

Chapter 12: Getting the Mastery of Body Language   87

    As A Speaker: 88

    As A listener: 90

Chapter 13: Body Language Analysis in Serious Relationships   93

Chapter 14: Effective Analysis of Body Language   99

Chapter 15: Body Language Mistakes To Avoid   104

Conclusion   108

Introduction

Learning about How to Analyze People often take a wide array of discussions and reading, many of which will cover multiple topics. In the course of this discussion, we need to know about the emergence of body language, its flexibility and its journey of transition from the beginning of human civilization till today. Body language is an excellent way of implicit conversation, where everything may not be spoken, yet it is explicable and understandable. So if you have never thought about this angle of conversation, here is the right time to bring this topic into the limelight.

Thank you for downloading *"How to Analyze People"*. All over the ensuing text of this book you will have a look upon the plentiful information on the subject matter of the body language, its persistence over the history and the extraordinary uses which emerged over the time. All this is realistically vital to be in your acquaintance if you wish to gain all the essential mastery of nonverbal communication.

But the story straight away extends the pace throughout the chapters. The grounds of direction towards preface information are very logical. It is probable to make up all of the readers wholly recognizable with the deliberation of the topic.

The various forms of nonverbal communication, with special reference to body language have been the point of focus in this book. Various types of body gestures and their respective uses have been touched in detail, so that all types of readers can find it constructive for their scrupulous rationale. A great deliberation has been contracted, to the role of body language in dissimilar and varying types of cultures. It is because body language is such a varied attitude that it also extends towards formal as well as informal communication. Some highly effectual steps have been suggested to make body language a perfect mode of success in all types of gatherings and communication platforms. In the end, various skill sets have been discussed to attain the mastery in this arena of communication.

Chapter 1:
Language- The Nonverbal Canvas

Man is a social entity. He cannot live without interacting or communicating with other beings, which is surrounding him. The history of language is as old as that of humans. Although the present day language may have unlimited number of alterations, transitions and modification, yet the common point between the contemporary and the historical language is their use as a source of communication and expression.

In the old civilizations, the language was not that developed as in modern day, but even in those days, it helped the mankind in forming the civilizations. It served as the foundation of forming the human civilizations and colonies. Whenever the anthropology or any other field of cultural study, start the research on any tribe or culture, language serves as the most significant characteristics which portrays the history of that meticulous culture. Nearly all the tribes around the globe strive hard to conserve their identity by taking precautionary measures for the survival of their language. As long the last man on earth will stay, so long will the language. It is not a mere amalgamation of words and texts, it entails a whole set of identity.

The canvas of unspoken words:

Man is considered among those creatures which has the highest form of intellect and astuteness. Although the sciences of linguistics believe that every group of creatures use some form of language, yet the humans are privileged to have a set of systematic linguistic framework. Now, as man has started his journey of development and put his steps forward, he has added a number of different aspects of language. People are now having multilingual approaches. The main purpose of this approach is to unite all mankind and become part of a larger group of people.

But when the highest extent of human intellect was attained, the consequence was the approval of nonverbal communication and language. It is a wider spectrum of human language, where unspoken is easily understood by the viewer. Many debates were conducted to judge that whether on verbal communication is a part of language, and the experts declared that it is not only a subsection of linguistics, rather it has the strongest power of expression and communication.

Nonverbal communication is subjected to a multiple number of realities and preferences. Although it is subjected to a variable number of interpretations yet it is powerful source of communication.

The power of implicit:

Owing to the nonverbal communication, language can be categorized into implicit and explicit. The explicit is easily communicated through various means of texts, phrases, and words. The implicit is hidden yet conveyed. It includes gestures and body language, which endorses the messages in a unique and convincing way.

But the implicit is as powerful as the explicit. The user can convey a wide number of issues and agendas within few gestures.

The supremacy of communication:

Long ago, there was a much-heated debate on the issue that whether nonverbal language, especially the body language can sustain the responsibility of communication. But as a result of in-depth examination, it was found that, not only statement, body language can serve a number of various purposes.

The body language governs the whole human body and makes the whole party involved in the process of conveying the message. The depth of meaning conveyed by the body language is still a question. It is also vulnerable to get molded, owing to a number of different interpretations. Body language can say a lot, even what is unspoken through a simple collection of words.

If used in a significant and useful way, the body language can solve a number of different puzzles encountered in the process of communication and sense making. The idiom articulated by the body parts hold permanent and enduring impressions. So if you want to become a perfect speaker, who can communicate and sustain a vast audience, you need to get mastery in the field of body language. Body language is more like an art, where you learn to make utmost use of your body parts.

Significance of the nonverbal canvas

a) Expression of emotions:

Emotions are better expressed than talked about. It is hard to tell someone how unhappy you feel and even if you do, they may not know just how unhappy you are until you show it. Some people tell a different thing than what they feel and so, it could be hard for you to understand their actual feelings until you read the nonverbal cues. Nonverbal communication is the best way to express your emotions. It is better understood by people who can already understand body language and so they are able to understand just how you feel.

Some of the emotions expressed nonverbally are:

Crying- This can either mean you are happy or sad. Intense excitement can make one cry as well as too much sorrow or sadness. Crying can also mean pretense and a need for sympathy, or even a cry for help. Depending on the person expressing the emotions and the situation and context, you can easily understand what the body language means.

Anger: It's impossible for one to start explaining how angry they are; you can only see it through their eyes and body language. Widened eyes, an open mouth, a down-turned mouth are among the tell-tale signs that one is actually angry. If the angry person crosses their hands, it means that they do not want you to approach them and so, you are better off staying away from them at that time.

Anxiety: This is another emotion that is easily expressed through body language. Increased blinking, some facial movements and a mouth stretched into a thin line are some of the expressions that can tell you that someone is anxious. Fidgeting is also something that you can watch out for as well as restlessness.

Pride: A proud person is easy to spot. Hands on the hips is a sign of pride, as well as someone tilting their head back when you are talking to them. Other people express pride through a small smile.

Embarrassment: An embarrassed person will not be able to face you. They will avert their eyes away from you they can even shift to face the other side. They will try their best to control their smile. If you are talking to someone and they are constantly looking down, it may be because they are embarrassed, they feel timid, or they are extremely shy.

Depending on what you are talking about, it can be very easy to know what the person is feeling at that moment.

Happiness/joy: It is very easy to know when a person is happy, even without talking to them. They will be smiling, jumpy, with eyes sparkling.

These are just a few emotions that people express better through nonverbal communication. It is good to be on the lookout for them if you want to communicate effectively with the other person.

b) Determining identities

When a person is trying hard to hide who they really are, it is easy to figure out the truth about them through their body language. The body does not lie, not like words. If you are keen enough, you can tell a person's personality and intentions much more easily through their body language. Watch what they say and how they say it; observe their eyes, their facial expressions, movement of their arms and anything else that will help you determine the true identity of a person.

Can it be faked?

Generally speaking, body language cannot be faked. This is due to the congruence that has to be there between spoken words, the main gestures as well as the body's small signals, which are also very significant. People who are able to read body language easily can tell when you fake it, and this will automatically mean that you are lying. To avoid being misunderstood, be as natural as you can. But in most cases, we exhibit body language unconsciously, which is another reason why it is hard to fake it.

Most adults especially men can easily fake their body language but children cannot. That explains why it is easier to read and understood body language of children more than that of adults. Besides, children have fewer muscle tones in their face therefore it makes is easier to know if they are genuine, lying, happy, sad, or even worried.

It is Easy to Misread Body Language

Many times people judge others according to their behavior on the first meeting. The first impression is used to pass judgment on the person, and it can be hard for you to change that opinion unless if you interact with the person a lot more times in the future. Misreading body language is very easy, and you could make a false judgment on the person if you are not careful.

A weak handshake, for instance, means that someone is not confident, or they have a weak personality especially if it is a man. If this person has arthritis on their hand, for instance, you do not expect their handshake to be firm and so, you will judge them without knowing the actual reason for sure.

Rules for Accurate Body Language Reading

As it has been earlier noted, it will be easy to misinterpret body language especially if you use a certain situation or incident to read a person's body language. However, if you follow these rules, you may arrive at the right decisions after all:

a) **Read gestures in clusters**: You are likely to make a mistake if you use only one gesture to interpret body language without involving all the other body gestures. If a person scratches their head, for instance, it can mean so many things but the actual meaning can be derived from associating that act with other gestures that occur at the same time with the main gesture. Gestures come in sentences called clusters; you have to read the entire sentence in order to understand the actual meaning of that particular gesture.

b) **Read gestures in context**: Gestures should be considered in the context within which they occur. A person that is seated or standing outside with arms crossed may be feeling cold, but one in a meeting with arms crossed may be blocking the conversation. Do not generalize one meaning for all similar gestures. A person crying and speaking loudly may be excited and not sad. A person smiling but speaking in low tones may be sad, but they want to show you that everything is alright.

c) **Always look for congruence**: Verbal and nonverbal languages should be in agreement. If for instance someone tells you that they agree with you but their facial expression shows something different, the best interpretation would be the body language. If the two are congruent, you can take their word for it. Someone who tells you they like you yet their arms are crossed in front of them may mean that they are not genuine; the truth of the matter is that they do not like you so much.

Chapter 2:
The Cultural Dimensions of Body Language

As far as the communication is concerned, it becomes trickier when the speaker and the listener belong to varying cultures. Some people are well aware of theses cultural differences. Therefore they make sure that they learn all kinds of cultures in which they have to move around.

Some of the cultural features pertaining to body language and nonverbal communication are discussed here to make sure that the learning of body language is complete from all respects.

Head Nodding:

Across varying cultures, Nodding of the head may refer to the diverse meanings from agreement to acknowledgment. The customary reply to a conclusion with which the other party or group of people do not agree is mostly showed through quiet gestures. No compliance is uttered erratically. Sometimes nodding connotes that although the other party is listening yet not agrees, however, in some cultures, both listening and agreement is showed through nodding of the head. So in case of any misunderstanding you can ask more than once so that the answer becomes clear. Sometimes open-ended questions may be helpful.

Head Shaking:

Head shaking is one of the first signs that we learn how to make as we are growing. It is the universal symbol of now, and we often do it instinctively without thinking about what we are doing. In most cultures, it is used when trying to say something without speaking, but many other cultures, especially in the Western world, us it while they are speaking to reinforce their statements.

Touch:

There are a number of customary values about touching while communicating. In some cultures, it is acceptable while in others it is highly forbidden. In the countries where it is not acceptable include, Germany, Australia, Portugal, Scandinavia, and England. The areas where touch is acceptable include Middle East, Asia, Russia, France and Turkey. However, this touching can also vary from gender to gender across cultures.

There is an entire section dedicated to touch, called Haptics, that we will focus on later within this guide.

The V sign

In many cultures, the V sign connotes variable meanings. It was originated by Winston Churchill, who used it in the Second World War as an emblem of victory. Some cultures believe that the palm facing towards the speaker refers to an insult. As such, the victory sign must be used with great care.

Sitting postures:

In Middle Eastern cultures, it is referred to as a kind of insult if the speaker or even the listener sits with cross legs or leg over the knee, with the sole of the shoe pointing towards the other person. While in European cultures it is a common sitting posture of the corporate sector.

Greeting:

A number of greeting gestures are prevalent all over the world. It varies from simple handshake to kissing on the cheeks or even hugging. In Middle Eastern and brain cultures, the meeting partners always greet each other with kisses on both cheeks while in European cultures handshake in more prevalent. In Asian cultures, both the partners continue holding hands, even for several minutes; it refers to the regard and affiliation. In European norms, the handshake is repetitive, at the start as well as at the end of the meeting. In some cultures like in Chinese provinces, the greeting is done by bowing in front of the partner, to depict respect and love. In many cultures, it is referred as insulting.

Dominance in conversations:

Italians will raise their hands high when speaking to show that they are in control of the conversation. This is different in countries like Germany, where people look as if they are paralyzed even when they are dominating the conversation. In the presence of Italians, Germans will not get a chance to dominate unless the hands of the Italian are held down. To dominate a conversation, a German may decide to touch the other party, a gesture which too many people is a show of affection. If you are not keen on these cultural differences, you may misunderstand the body language in the end.

Stiff-upper Lip:

Many people purse their lips in order to control their face so as to reveal little or no emotions in an interaction. In England, this is a show that you are in total control of your emotions. Some cultures may interpret this as lack of emotions on your part especially if you do it in an emotional situation and they may take offense at that. In some cultures, a stiff-upper-lip can be used to show a feeling of intimidation.

Smiley nods:

In Japan, smiley nods are cues to let the other person know that you are listening and that they may continue talking. This is accompanied mainly by polite noises. Europeans and Westerners have the smiley nods as well but to them, it is a show of agreement. When a Japanese person is encouraging you to go on talking, a Westerner will think that he is actually agreeing with you every step of the way.

One thing for sure is that cultural basics pertaining to body language are the same everywhere. Facial expressions for instance smiles and frowns are the same everywhere, and they carry the same meanings. Actually, expressions of disgust, happiness, surprise and sadness are the same in many countries. In the case of other expressions you are not sure about, it is better to take time and learn about them first to avoid misinterpreting body language.

Chapter 3:
Haptics

Haptics, as we have already mentioned, has to do with touching. The word "haptics" comes from the Greek word that means "I touch," and has to do with the sense of touch most medical, biological or technological applications - haptics in technology.

Touch is one of the best ways that we have to communicate with other people, and it will always be, not matter how much technology we have. Many would even go out of their way to say that touch is actually one of the most, if not the most, basic communication tools that human beings and even some animals have.

> **Think about it: is there a more direct and intimate way to interact with our world than using touch?**

Haptics, while it is not quite as popular as other types of body language, is closely related to another study that is much more popular: Proxemics, or the study of space in body language. In both cases, the person has to understand and be able to interpret personal space and territory, and the fine line that exists between too much and not enough. Touch is usually the direct result of allowing others into our intimate space, so it goes hand in hand with this type of study. We obviously wouldn't allow others to touch us if we don't feel comfortable being around them.

In this section we are going to delve into Haptics and talk about what makes it an essential part of body language, what advantages you can get by using touch in your body language, why to include it in your daily readings of situations and people, and how to implement it in your communication. We will also take a closer examination at some common ways to be "in touch" with others and their meanings. Remember that touch does not always involved the hands, but can include everything from the top of your head to the tips of your toes.

So what is so special about touch and Haptics?

There are two very unique qualities and specializations to Haptics that distinguish it from most other types of body language and communication styles:

Number 1: Our sense of touch is the most genuine or "real" method that we have to sense and understand the world and those around us. Sometimes it can be hard for us to believe that something or someone is actually real, that is unless we can actually touch and feel it with our own bodies – even if we can see it. It is just something that dates back to our heritage and culture. So while we tend to take it mostly for granted, our sense of touch should not be taken lightly by any of us. Instead, we should celebrate that it is something that we can use to our advantage.

Number 2: Simply put: without our sense of touch and feeling, we wouldn't be able to understand body language at all. You will soon see why.

Imagine living in a world where you couldn't touch or sense anything. You could still use your hands to do things, but you really wouldn't be connected to it, no matter what it is: dirty laundry, a baby, or your dinner. Of course there are some good things as well, you won't feel pain when you cut yourself or if you get burned. There are some diseases where people actually can't feel, and it has led to a lot of problems for them.

So why is touch important?

Without the sense of touch or feeling, we would actually have deep, deep psychological problems. We would feel isolated and helpless, even if we were surrounded by people. As humans, we feel and understand with every square inch of our skin. Some, like the bottoms of our feet, we don't even think about while others, like our fingertips, we do. It allows us to feel heat and cool through the largest organ that makes up our body.

Every second of the day, we receive an endless stream of information about our environment, all from the way our skin reacts to it. In fact, it is so important to use that studies have shown that babies who lack a sense of touch have a very, very low chance of survival in contrast to the lack of other senses like sight or hearing. If they don't develop the skills to feel touch, it is nearly impossible to work with them on a psychological level. That's probably why it's the first sense we develop when we're embryos.

In short - touch is the initial and most basic form of communication we have as humans and animals.

The Emotions of Touch

Touch is, along with being an essential type of communication, a very emotional type of communication that many people take for granted. You could even say that it's the most human type of body language that we have. In a sense, it's like delivering our emotions in a physical form. There's probably no better way to comfort someone but to embrace them into a huge and hold onto them until they feel better, or no better way to show your disapproval with a person or a comment than with a sounding slap on the face. You feel will that, and so will they.

With these qualities in mind, it is then very easily understood that we're dealing here with something very "touchy" and sometimes something that is volatile – it's like an emotional dynamite. It's a strong communication tool, perhaps the strongest that we actually have, but if it's used improperly, it will backfire, and backfire hard. That is why so many people try to understand how to read it and how to use it to our advantage.

So you must understand how one communicates with touch and how one understands what exactly is being communicated:

What are the benefits of using touch with others?

You must first understand that most humans, notice we say most but definitely not all, crave and want physical touch. We need that kind of communication to get through our daily lives: it is not something that we can just turn on and off.

When we fulfill that need, we get more healthy, happy and content in our lives. Here are some demonstrations of the power of touch:

1. Massages: massages aren't just a way to relieve stress and stop pain through expertly applied pressure. Instead it is a natural thing that prevents diseases and high blood pressure. How? Just the touch of another human being speeds up our immune system.

2. Touch is a way to express physical intimacy between two people. It doesn't matter if these two people are friends, lovers, or family members. It creates a bond that we all yearn for.

3. Touch is a comfort tool; that's why we use it even to comfort ourselves. Many people do something called "self-touch" or comforting themselves. This is a method that astronauts and soldiers who are going on a mission alone will use to help themselves stay in a positive frame of mind.

4. Touch can actually serve as an amplifier for every message you send. Simply touching someone's shoulder or grabbing someone's hand can mean more than saying calming and soothing words. You are reinforcing what you are saying with the simplest touch. Of course it's a double edged sword if you use it in the wrong way: if someone has trouble trusting you, for example, you can just reinforce that feeling by touching that person in a way that makes them feel uncomfortable. That is why you have to use other forms of body language to full understand touch.

5. The last, but not least, thing that you need to consider about your sense of touch is that this is probably the most efficient tool for creating bonds and rapport with other people and animals in your life. Be it in a physical or intimate relationships, a working relationships, or a parent-child relationship, a soft touch says, "I care for you and want to be in contact." The physical connection often establishes the emotional connection.

You have to know when and where to touch a person. It often has to do with knowing that person on a new level rather than just understanding their body language. You have to know the person. If you do, touch is invaluable in creating and strengthening connections. Do it right and you can build trust and credibility, do it wrong and get yourself slapped.

Types of Touch

Keep in mind that these examples are by no means the only ways you can communicate by touch – we will explore some of the other types of touch within the next few chapters of this guide. We recommend, as always, that you explore and experiment by yourself to truly understand Haptics and body language. What you learn in theory will stay a theory unless you try it out.

Hugging it Out

Can you think of a feeling that is better when you are upset than a nice warm hug from someone you know cares about you? While it's pretty straightforward in its meaning, there are some subtexts and deviations to hugging.

Hugging, which is similar to kissing and we will get to that next, is a ritual that has been with humans since the dawn of time. No one is really sure where or why we started, just that we have. For many, we think that it is instinctual.

It's one of the things that makes us human though some other primates hug as well. As we are social creatures, we have grown and evolved because we have the ability to communicate and cooperate with others – something that we might not always use as much as we should. We are genetically wired to be surrounded by others and make physical contact with them - **it's strengthening our bonds and making us healthier and happier.**

Kissing

Kissing is slightly more complicated than hugging, but it is also a necessary part of body language. In fact, kissing actually started as something much more utilitarian than hugging – it most likely evolved from the mouth feeding that we see a mother bird do to her child. But unlike animals, we humans adapted this gesture to serve other forms, and that's why we have so many kiss types.

Still, it's a bit murky as to why we actually started kissing at all. It's a question that has plagued us for generations, so much so that there is actually a whole research field that is dedicated simply to finding why we kiss, studying the kiss, and understanding how it affects us: Philematology.

So far, there really hasn't been about breakthroughs, at least to the public, about the reason behind kissing or even putting our mouths closer to each other. We feed our young in a completely different way. A scientist might argue that it's part of the sexual activity and health of humans, just like sex is, so we don't really need to look any further for explanations. But that's not entirely correct because sex is something that we need to further the human species through connection and reproduction. We don't need to kiss in order to reproduce though some would argue that it at least adds to the experience. There are two sticking points in Philematology:

1. Yes, kissing is fun, there's really no biological necessity for it to exist, at least in today's world. **We can reproduce without kissing.**

2. Yeah, kissing is very popular today, but it wasn't evident much in cultures outside the western civilization a few decades ago – especially in romantic relationships. There has been more evidence about friendly kissing on the cheek between men than there is about kissing between lovers. Kissing became much more prominent as a result of the western culture spread around the world.

Holding Hands

From an early age, we hold onto the hands of our parents and teachers to lead us – it's the symbol of unity and trust.

But how to hold hands, and with whom it's acceptable? This can widely differ in many parts of the world.

Romantic Hand Holding

The most obvious meaning for holding hands with someone else is the involvement of romance.

You see it everywhere you go: from the opera to the grocery store – men and women holding hands to keep themselves connected. It is one of those momentous "firsts" that we have in our relationship. Especially when we are younger, it is seen as the "big step" toward forwarding a relationship. Insignificant and stupid as it might feel in an older, more modern relationship, it was probably your first attempt in building romantic physical intimacy.

Is interlocking fingers a more sustainable, stable relationship?

Generally speaking, at least from a body language perspective, yes, it's more physically and emotionally bonding than simply walking hand in hand with your hands cupped. But it doesn't apply to everyone, some people just uncomfortable doing it. This is especially true in people who work more manual labor jobs, as they have tougher hands, and relationships where there is a large size difference.

Support, Strength, Guidance, and Authority

Another use that we have for holding hands, especially for those that are young (or older) than us is to guide and protect those who are less able to lead themselves or those who aren't as confident as we are:

> We take our children by the hand to lead them down paths or across streets so that they won't get lost.

> We support older people in their walks, especially across unstable terrain. Or help a blind man cross the street.

> The hand is a safety net that allows them to feel comfortable and protected – allowing them to go out on a limb.

> We take someone by the hand when we pass through the crowd so we won't get separated, giving comfort to both parties.

> When offering our hand for support when our loved ones feel threatened or distressed.

Hand-holding isn't appropriate in some situations, including within the business sphere.

Chapter 4:
When is it Appropriate to Touch?

Some people have a problem knowing when or when not to touch someone or something else. While many of us can manage on our own, when we start paying too much attention to body language, we sometimes start to forget our manners. Appropriate touch really means something different to nearly everyone, and is defined by a lot of things that are unique and personal. You aren't likely to know that you are making someone uncomfortable unless they tell you, but touch the wrong person, the wrong part of the body or in an improper time and your reputation is at risk, or it's just an invitation for a really awkward moment.

The main thing you need to focus on is getting your judgment right. You need to learn how to read how and where you can touch someone. Only then will you be able to understand how someone reacts when you touch them.

So what exactly we can communicate through touch?

Touch, as you have already read, is a specific type of communication that based on context, communication, relationship, culture, and many other small details. This means that different situations and characters can significantly alter the meaning of the touch that you give. A pat on the back can suggest encouragement in one scenario and a signal to get attention in another. Think about something as simple as fist shake, it can mean something so different to so many people.

As such - touch is a very versatile tool that we have been given in person to person contact. We adopt it in many ways in our interactions, depending upon the situation. So how to do we use touch:

> We can use it to comfort others

> To comfort ourselves

> To convey affection or make a move

> To create a bond between groups of people

> To get someone's attention

> To direct and guide someone or something

> To greet someone formally or informally

> To ask for an advice

> To "tease" playfully

> To show ownership

Touch can be great, no? Still, if we ignore the social codes around a specific greeting or touch, we send a message that can land us in trouble. Remember that until you have established a certain relationship, most forms of touching should be avoided. If you have to greet someone, a handshake is the best option. If you aren't even sure if that is appropriate, wait for that person to make the first move.

What do we need to consider before touching?

If we want the message in our touch to pass through and be perceived correctly by the other party, the giver of the touch needs to understand how they think, and how they might perceive it. That person needs to put themselves in the shoes of that person. If we don't really know the person that we are about touch, then we cannot always accurately predict how they will respond to us, but we can minimize our mistakes by taking into consideration the factors in play. At the end of the day, minimizing those mistakes can really pay off – especially in the business world.

The factors that determine the "rules" of touching are quite similar to those that affect Proxemics. It's not a surprise, haptics are very familiar subjects in nonverbal communication. Many companies will train their employees on these different topics, especially when they go abroad or travel to new cultures.

Let's take a look at some of the ways that haptics and body language are impact:

> **Note: The discussions within this manual will focus mostly on the relationship between Western cultures and the rest of the world. While that is not the only important culture to discuss, information is much freer in this culture.**

Gender

We live in a society where gender has a more important and less important role. However, it is still huge when it comes to determining how to touch someone, where to touch someone, and when to touch someone.

As a general rule, those who identify as female are more comfortable with touching than those who identify as male. This could be due to their maternal role, or it could just be due to social conditioning. Males, as a rule, prefer more businesslike touches that are brief. This could be because they don't want to be perceived as anything less than manly.

If you don't really believe that, all you have to do is go to your local mall and take a look at the contrast between female and male friends. Women will usually have much more comfort and freedom to touch each other: they hug upon meeting each other, they link arms, and sometimes they even hold hands. They will comfort each other, snuggle together, and generally just touch more often and without thinking about it. Men, however, will immediately start to feel very weird and pull away quickly if a hug lasts a second longer than they think it should, and we will automatically suspect that something is wrong. They also maintain a larger personal bubble, which almost eliminates the risk of unconscious touching.

When it comes to the type of touching that is allowed between opposite sexes and genders, it's a walk on thin ice, there's almost always the sexual subtext in the background. Even if the two people aren't attracted to each other, there can still be problems. That is a societal issue that hopefully we will solve, but so far we have not been able to get an answer.

Men, especially cis gendered straight men, have a tendency to interpret female touch, especially if given freely and without thought, as a sexual advance, whether it's true or not. It is something that is engrained in the collective male mind from years and years of conditioning. It could also be because men are less used to touch, so they think that almost every other touch has a deeper meaning. Women, who are used to being with female friends, often give these touches without second thought. Male touch often interpreted as powerful, paternal and dominant.

This common distinction between the role of touch in each gender leads to many social misinterpretations that have caused trouble for both genders. Emotionally and physically for women, and socially and politically for men. For example, it leaves women in powerful yet vulnerable position. If a male boss touches a female on the back, it can be viewed as a sexual advance. This could land the male in deep trouble, and even cost him his job.

When a man touches a woman, it is typically to show dominance or power. Touching between couples is display of ownership, and it's common for young couples who cling to each other.

If you are a man, you have to know when it is appropriate to touch a female. You should also know that just because she touches you on the arm, which does not give you permission to touch her inappropriately.

Difference in Cultures

Different cultures have different codes when it comes to the amount of touch that is socially acceptable and how it should be done. We have already talked about this is another section, but touch needs to be discussed by itself, as it can be vitally important. Usually you can just follow the lead of someone else, but sometimes you will be all by yourself and not know what is appropriate. That's why it's important to check the local customs when visiting foreign countries to avoid offending or be offended by the locals.

For example, if you travel somewhere that you have never been, you might inadvertently offend someone. You can do this in any number of ways, from the symbols that use (the peace sign means something different in other cultures), the way you eat (in some cultures, if you don't belch, you didn't enjoy the meal), and even the way you hold yourself (in some cultures, you need to let women walk in front of you).

Status and Authority

The act of touching someone else is usually initiated by active side of the interaction and not vice versa. Think about when you touch someone that isn't a romantic or a familial bond:

- ➢ You ask a favor

- ➢ Give directions or information

- ➢ Give an order

- ➢ When you're trying to persuade someone

- ➢ When you have something to share

- ➢ When you want to comfort someone

You rarely touch someone else when you're in a passive or weak position. In fact, we often curl up and resist touch when we feel weak. That's why dominant and authoritative figures usually initiate touch. Because leadership is about action, not sitting by and waiting.

Also, just like in terms of personal space, touch is related to hierarchy - influential people have more permission to touch others, due to their position or role. For a lower status to touch a higher status is considered as inappropriate, sleazy or bold behavior. Though it is a lowbrow example, think about being at a strip club: it is inappropriate for you to touch the stripper, but the stripped can touch you.

For a more highbrow example, it's okay for the doctor to touch you to check your organs, but it's not cool for you to touch the doctor.

How to Implement Touching in Body Language?

So now you know when and where it is appropriate to touch someone. But how are we going to use touch in body language to our advantage? How can we use touch without digging ourselves into a deep hole? Do we need to start touching people randomly and hopefully get a positive response?

Let's delve in further:

Initiate Touch

Before we can even think about touching someone, we need to work on establishing some sort of personal connection with them. Even the simplest greeting that we have already talked about– the handshake, is only truly appropriate after prolonged eye contact. It should also go along with a vocal greeting and continued eye contact. Try to do this the other way around and see what happens – you are likely to get out on the wrong foot. Remember that first impressions do last.

The more intimate the relationship, if you are on a date versus if you are in a business meeting – the more touching is allowed and to the more private parts. It's only logical because we need to trust and like someone before we give them a "free access" to our more personal zones.

> ➤ Note: You need to be given explicit permission to touch someone in places that are considered private. Remember that you need to ask the person, and that person needs to be in a clear frame of mind for consent.

So far – so good, but does it matter who initiates the contact?

Who can initiate contact?

Why yes it does!

Like was mentioned in the first part of this guide and repeated throughout (which means that it is very important) – touch is something that's usually initiated by the higher status and active persona. That is typically determined by gender identity, but it doesn't always have to be. Be it to give a command or to comfort – the person who initiates the contact is the one steering the wheels. That's why if it's important for you to be in control or to appear more active, you should strive to initiate the touch. You should also consider looking into the reasons why you need to feel in control, just to make sure that it comes from a positive place.

If you look at politicians, for example, you'll notice that there's a certain power struggle when they meet and greet each other – each one will try to appear as the dominant figure by using a pat on the back, a two handed handshake or using his hands to guide someone. That is because we still look at touch and body language to determine who the "better" option is – even if we don't realize that is what we are doing. It's all for the show obviously.

Be careful though, it's often a bad idea to make the first move with your superiors, because it will be perceived as ambitious and inappropriate. You don't want to send off the wrong message. This is especially true if your superior is a man.

Touch is an Amplifier

One of the most important parts of body language is the timing with which we use it. It's the use of matching verbal and nonverbal communication in the right time. You have to learn how to read those facial tics and movements – we will go in depth with those later. There is a congruency, grace and natural flow to things that if you disrupt, you might cause damage to your reputation and relationship.

Influential figures know that and they use touch in body language to emphasize their messages – they understand that just shifting their hands from one place to another can really change things. They know how to push the right buttons at the right moments to amplify their message tenfold.

So how is it done? Well, it is something that takes quite some time to learn – but simply by reading this book, you are starting to learn the basics that you can then build on. A lot of it is trial and error. A lot of it is watching the masters. Look online for motivational speakers or watch movies with master actors, and you will see how they hold themselves. These actors have put in the leg work to really change the way they hold themselves.

For example, watch the movie *The Devil Wears Prada*. Look at how Meryl Streep, one of the best actresses of all time, holds herself in her role as Miranda Priestly. You see that she changes the way she holds her body when she is interacting with different people. When she is talking to her assistants, she holds herself one way, when she is talking to designers, she holds herself another way. Watch and try to mimic those movements. Then, make it natural for the way you hold yourself.

You might not be Meryl Streep, but this is one of those situations where you need to fake it until you make it.

Determine the Approachability of the Person you will touch

When meeting with strangers or associates that you don't really know – it's always hard to know when it is okay to touch them, and when you should just keep your hands to yourself. Of course, it is best to follow the lead of someone who might know better, but that isn't always appropriate.

To help you determine if someone is "touchable" you need to seek signs of approachability:

➢ Open body language

➢ Keeping eye contact

➢ Smiling

➢ Nodding

➢ The first move

➢ A step forward

You can also look at how this person interacts with some of the other people in the room. Look for these signs:

➢ Does he use touch and accepts it?

➢ Is he smiling?

➢ How does he greet others?

➢ Does he use gestures a lot?

This type of person most likely will welcome some form of touch. On the other hand:

- ➤ Is he frowning?

- ➤ Does he have his arms crossed?

- ➤ Are his hands clasped behind his back?

- ➤ Is he not making a move?

There's a good chance he won't accept a stranger's touch.

Next Question: Where to Touch?

It's a hard question, and the answer really depends on the situation. Still, the basic answer is to always err on the side of caution.

As a general rule, you want to make sure that your contact feels casual, neutral, inoffensive, and brief if that's someone you barely know. Remember that by touching someone, even if it is just their hand, you invade their personal space for a moment, and if they don't like it or trust you enough yet – your touch would feel alien and unpleasant for them. Be as gentle as you can – you never know if someone has a problem with touch or pressure.

No matter where you are, it's better to leave a slightly less passionate impression that an over enthusiastic one. Remember, touch in body language is like dynamite – you don't want to push it too hard. Also, even a light and brief touch can do wonders to improve your interaction and leave a memorable impression.

You know where is appropriate and where isn't appropriate to touch people, especially people of the opposite gender. Use your head and remember that impressions can be deadly.

Where not to touch?

The more precise question that you should ask is: "Where is it not appropriate to touch, especially if I'm not sure?"

The parts of the body that would be blurred on television, especially around the genital area, are guarded with most vigilance and, therefore, are 'off limits' to strangers. If the intimacy grows these parts may be put within your reach – BUT YOU STILL HAVE TO ASK.

Another part you should generally avoid touching is the head of adults. Even in cultures where it's not a taboo to touch the head, it's still considered a condescending gesture. Many people, especially women, are also self-conscious about their hair. That isn't to say that men aren't either – can you image going to touch someone's head and coming back with his wig?

The best thing you can do with touching is limit it until you know you are free to do something else. While this might seem cold to you, it will help you in the long run.

Chapter 5:
Eye Contact

Throughout the chapters we have covered so far, you have heard about the importance of eye contact. Eye contact is a part of body language that is sometimes overlooked, but is critical when you want to use it. To be proficient in using body language and eye contact, you must know:

➤ What makes the eyes the center of attention?

➤ How to make eye contact?

➤ How long to hold it?

➤ What are the different kinds of eye contact?

➤ How to know if someone is uncomfortable with eye contact?

➤ Can you tell if someone is lying by eye contact?

➤ What do the pupils have to do with it?

You probably didn't know that you could find all of this out via eye contact, but you can. The eyes are the window to the soul as they say, and you can really tell what someone is about by gazing deep into their eyes.

Why are the eyes important?

Eyes, as we have said, show what we are really thinking and feeling. They have that necessary spark that makes us human. They are also something that, while we can control them, it is nearly impossible to do so without intense training.

Have you ever held eye contact and known immediately that you loved that person? That you hated them? Have you ever had a conversation with someone using only eye contact? It is possible.

This is because your eyes mirror neurons, which give us the ability of feeling empathy, love, hatred, fear, or even resentment towards each other and understand how others feel. While people can control their facial expressions or their body positioning, eyes are a different story.

How long should we hold eye contact?

Once again, this is a "situation by situation" case where it depends on where you are and what you are doing. Research suggests that maintaining eye contact between 60-70 percent of the time will allow someone to feel like they can trust you. Anything less, and you could come across as anything from untrustworthy to immature.

The ultimate goals is to make as much eye contact as you can – just as long as you feel comfortable enough to do so and without threatening the other person. But how can you tell if a person is comfortable? Once again, we turn to some questions:

- ➤ How well do know them?

- ➤ What is your relationship?

- ➤ What is their status to you?

- ➤ How many people are you looking at?

- ➤ Is it male or female?

- ➤ How close do you stand to that person?

➢ What is appropriate by culture and custom?

You might not always know the answers to these questions, but you should strive to find out what is appropriate. Follow the lead of others, do your research, or even ask someone near you.

A person's pupils will shrink if they feel threatened or scared, and they will grow if they see something they like. If worst comes to worst, you can use that as a guide.

Chapter 6:
Smiles and Laughter

Smiling and laughing have been universally accepted as body language that will show when a person is happy or excited. From birth, babies know that crying will call for attention but smiling will keep it there and at five weeks, they are able to smile. Smiling in humans shows that you are less threatening and that the other person can accept you on a personal level. Not smiling on the other hand is a way to show that you are less submissive, dominant, aggressive among others meanings.

Smiles and laughter are used by people differently and some of the smiles may not mean the positive things they are meant to show. You have to be careful when interpreting smiles and laughter so as to get the right meaning at all times.

Big smiles, showing your teeth produces a good reaction in other people. People are likely to smile back at you, and this creates harmony between you. This is much more different from a tight-lipped, no teeth showing smile. All these are smiles but they mean a different thing.

Smiles and laughter are another way through which people communicate nonverbally. Just like the touch, eye contact and distance, you can easily learn body language by understanding a person's laughter or smile.

The sincerity of a smile must be determined though since some smiles and laughter are fake and they can communicate something different from the genuine ones. Look out for the wrinkle lines beside the eyes and you will know if a smile is genuine or not.

Some of the meanings of smiles and laughter are:

> An enjoyment smile involves pulled up lip corners and contracted muscles around the eyes. Non-enjoyment smiles only involve the smiling lips, though the muscles around the eyes remain unchanged.

> If it is an apology, and it is accompanied with a smile, it is more significant than one without a smile. In courtrooms, for instance, the apology with a smile could attract lesser penalty than one without a smile.

Importance of smiles and laughter

> Smiling at people influences their attitude and how they react towards you.

> Smiling can bring positive results especially if used professionally.

> A smiling stranger may be friendly.

> A smile may assist the message that you are delivering especially in a conversation.

> It is hard to misunderstand a smiling person especially if the verbal message is not clear.

Fake Smiles

It may be very hard for some people to differentiate between fake smiles and genuine ones. A sincere smile will carry a positive message but when it is fake, you will interpret it negatively, and this can help you understand the smiling person better. Do not be content when someone is smiling at you because it may not be genuine after all. Look through their eyes and watch out for other body languages and the situation so that you can understand their behavior better.

Many people take advantage of the fact that smiling is a disarming gesture in order to use it when they are lying so as to get away with their lies. However, unconsciously someone lying will smile less than they always do and if you know then very well, you can easily tell that they are lying even if they are smiling.

A smile from a liar comes more quickly than a genuine person, and it lasts for a longer time. A liar has to exaggerate it in order to convince you but if you are keen enough, you will notice the different between that fake smile and the genuine one.

A fake smile is much stronger on one side of the face than the other. Watch out for this! When one is happy, both brain hemispheres work to send the message to both sides of the face, for a fake smile, only one side of the brain sends the message and only to one side of the face, which is why the other side of the face seems neutral during the smile. The left side of the face smiles more than the right side.

Types of smiles

Below is a summary and an analysis of the common types of smiles that you are likely to see every day:

> ➢ The tight-lipped smile: In this smile, the lips are stretched to form a straight line while the teeth are hidden. This smile could mean that the person smiling has something they are hiding and they are not willing to share it with you. It could be a secret, an attitude or an opinion that they would rather keep to themselves.

This is a smile used mostly by women when they come across someone that they do not like but they do not want the person to know. Women know that this is a rejection signal but most men do not know what it means.

➤ The sly smile: This is a smile on one side and something else on the other. It is a show of different emotions on both sides of the face. This smile shows sarcasm or contempt in most instances. There are people who smile this way though so if you know a person really well, you will may conclude that they are being sarcastic if they give you a sly smile.

➤ The drop jaw smile: In the smile, the lower jaw is completely dropped to show that the person is either laughing or playing. This is a smile of happiness and it is used mainly by people who want to show their happiness and gratitude to others. When people are having fun, this is the kind of smile you will expect. Watch out for the fake smiles though because there are people who can fake it.

➤ Sideways looking up smile: In this smile, the head is turned down and away while the person is looking up and smiling. This smiling person looks somehow secretive or even playful. Men love this kind of smile in women as it awakens their feelings to want to care and protect the woman. This is a smile that can touch the heart of people. You may want to like someone that smiles that way. During courtship, this is a smile that many take as seductive- it could mean to a man that you are signaling them to come so if you are looking for a suitor, this could be the smile to wear.

➢ A grin: A grin or a smirk could mean different things to a lot of people. Some people wear such smiles all the time in the presence of people just to show that they are not angry at anything. Some people will wear a grin on the face to show sarcasm or to mock another person. Depending on the situation one is at and the kind of person they are, you can easily interpret a grin.

A smiling person is often mysterious as you may not know what they have been up to even if you know them so well. Always take laughter and smiles seriously as some people laugh and smile even when they are not really feeling happy. All you need to do is look deeper, and watch their eyes. Their eyes will speak to you even if their smiles do not.

Chapter 7:
The Study of Proxemics

No study of body language would be complete without focusing on the whole of the body and where the body stands in relation to another person.

Proxemics, another sub category in the study of body language, is the name of the study that explains how people treat their space and other people in their proximity. It's a subcategory of our nonverbal communication, much like our eyes and touch. In fact, people who study touch often study proxemics as well.

Have you ever stopped to really think about how you move around others? How close to you get to someone? Why do you choose that seat on the train instead of another one? Or why do you choose to stand instead of sitting at all? Why did someone choose to sit next to you?

These small, daily, droll things that we do aren't random or "fate" like some would have you believe. Instead, we have a deeply engrained social code built in our collective subconscious that tells us where to sit, where to stand, and how far away to be from someone else's person.

Why It's Important

Depending on where you live, you will get closer to some people than you will others. If you take the subway in New York City, you are likely to get closer to people than someone who lives in the Midwest and has acres of land.

Still, you are likely to come into contact with people from all different walks of life, so understanding how to use your space and how others keep theirs is crucial in creating the right connections and leaving a good impression. Make a mistake here, and you can gravely insult or annoy someone that you really didn't even think twice about, and the worst part is that they probably won't even say anything.

Importance of Giving (and Having) Personal Space

The space we keep around ourselves has multiple purposes: mental clarity, safety, hygiene, privacy, and even sanity. Can you imagine touching someone all the time? You'd go crazy.

Most people don't take their personal space seriously until someone is seriously invading it. We all have a different size personal space, and a lot of the time it depends on the other person. Still, it is something that makes up and affects our social interactions to an extreme degree.

Cramping Someone's Space

Something that a lot of kindergarten teachers use to help students get along is the idea of a personal bubble. Think of the area around you as a bubble that saves you from hurt and dirt. We treat the few feet around us as our "private air space," and we feel very, very uncomfortable and vulnerable when someone intrudes it without invitation. Obviously, it's not the environmental hazards like rain or snow that we fear, but instead what kind of damage that other person can do by standing so close to us.

What happens inside when someone invades our personal space or bubble?

Our brains kind of go crazy when someone steps too close for comfort. It causes us to tighten up, go on high alert, and even causes physical reactions. We try to make ourselves smaller and we might start to sweat. However, it is the emotional reaction that causes the most problems, and it doesn't matter if we know the person or we don't. This goes for while we are in the supermarket or while we are in the board room:

- ➢ We become too self-aware of everything from our breathing to our scent and suddenly we forget how to act 'naturally'

- ➢ We start to read too much into our movements.

- ➢ We reduce eye contact.

- ➢ We curl in on ourselves and try to avoid eye contact, especially if we don't know the person.

- ➢ We'll usually immediately take a step back.

- ➢ We adopt a defensive position – folded arms, less smiles, frowning, tense posture.

- ➢ We stop having any conversations immediately.

Think about when you were little: did you and your siblings ever play that game where you stand with your hand really, really close to them, but you aren't touching? Typically you say something like "I'm not touching you, I'm not touching you!" This makes them uncomfortable. How do you know it makes them uncomfortable? Because it makes you feel the same way.

In short – space invasion is something we have noticed since we were very young and it puts us in a very uncomfortable and protective position. We can feel vulnerable and angry or it can even cause us to slowly become extremely paranoid.

This doesn't happen with everyone all of the time, but it does happen with everyone. Think about your significant other, is there ever a time when you just don't want them to touch you? It usually has nothing to do with something that they did, and everything to do with how you feel.

Why does this happen?

Our sense of personal space is extremely complex and varies from person to person. The factors that contribute to the size are actually a cause of social implications and interactions, when different people have a different concept about the 'right distance' to stand from each other. Some of these factors are:

➢ Where you are at the present time

➢ Who that person is to you

➢ How others will feel about the contact

➢ What your emotions are toward the other person

➢ What gender you are

➢ Culture– perhaps the most major factor.

Different cultures have their own measurement of the 'right' personal space. While many in the Western World have similar thoughts, they can even vary from place to place. Think about a place like New York City – someone standing close to you on the subway isn't a big deal, but someone following closely behind you on the street might cause the hairs on the back of your neck to stand up. Mainly, it has to do with:

➢ Intention

➢ The density of our living space

So with so many different ideas about what and when and where these bubbles are, how can you determine what is the best way to get close to someone, even if it is within a few feet?

You can look at their body language: do they appear to be comfortable? You can also use some of those defining characteristics that we have discussed in previous chapters. Of course, the reasons behind personal bubbles vary from person to person for many things, but here is just a hint:

Gender

Women are, traditionally, much more sociable than men are: they understand the importance of social cues better, are much more emotionally expressive than men, and tend to communicate their emotions better. Therefore, naturally women feel more comfortable being closer to each other.

Men, on the other hand, are far more territorial than women tend to be, and couple with their aggressive nature and fear of coming across as inferior, tend to keep the distance from each other. However, that all changes when they get near a woman: they tend to get closer and closer.

However, that works in reverse for women: they tend to be more uncomfortable around men and want to take a few steps back. This is due to societal pressures and collective memories.

Culture

The culture that we identify with is one of the biggest causes of our personal bubble. It affects whether or not we like someone to be close to us. In fact, it directly influences our space based on what we are used to. Studies have shown that even people who like a lot of personal space like it in proportion to where they are from. Meaning, that someone from Beijing who likes a lot of personal space still likes less personal space than someone from Alaska.

'Distant' cultures, like those found in northern Europe, US, and many other westerns cultures, tend to keep more personal space between just about everyone and use less touching (Haptics) than other more 'warm' cultures that encourage touch.

These warm cultures include Asian cultures (think back to that Beijing examples) because they are characterized by more accommodating accepting attitude when it comes to personal space, the theory says it's due to more crowded living conditions.

Other cultures that are considered to be warm and need less personal space include south Europe, Middle East and South American's. Standing closer to someone or sitting closer is considered to be a "normal" part of life.

Isn't this all just one big stereotype?

Obviously, we are generalizing this information, and to take it as the hard and fast truth would be a big mistake. That isn't to say that all Asians are warm and all Europeans are cold and horrible people. It is simple a way to remember the social cues of a specific place or area.

Don't let these generalizations about personal space affect you judgment of other cultures either, like Einstein said – "it's all relative." How much personal space you need has absolutely nothing to do with what type of person you are. Sometimes it is all about warming up to someone, and sometimes people just really don't like to be touched.

When arriving to a foreign country or a business you don't really know anything about, it would be smart to adjust yourself to the cultural codes of personal space of the place. Don't try to make people adjust for you. If you are in the minority, you need to adjust for that specific person.

There's also a difference between country living culture and the urban city lifestyle – country people are used to live in a vast and mildly populated areas while city dwellers are more used to crowding. This means that city dwellers will usually have a smaller personal space than country people due to this habit of density.

Status

Your status in any given situation is something that has one of the biggest impacts on the amount of personal space that you need to have and the amount of personal space that you need to give. First of all – like the alpha male of the pack, the higher a person's status is, the more personal space that person needs. It's no surprise that the first class seats are bigger and have more space per individual, as those people are deemed to be more important than those of us who sit in coach.

Status not only affects the size you get, but the size you require. People who are higher on the totem pole tend to move with more determination, swinging their arms or taking larger steps, thus entitling them to more space. Think about people who have a lot of money, they have bigger homes because they need more space for all of their things. This is something that hasn't changed for years and years, and is likely to stay the same for the next few centuries.

When it comes to dominant – subordinate relationships, it means that the high status person can invade the space of the lower status person without really crossing a line. While it might not seem that way to the person who is lower, in truth it really doesn't matter. It is a sad reality about our social construct, but it is an overarching construct nonetheless.

For example, if you are building a hotel for a very important businessman, he can lean down in your face and look at the blueprints while you are talking, but if you get really close to him while he is looking, you are overstepping and might just get yourself fired from that particular job.

Obviously, this rule applies even if you don't really like the person of the higher status. In fact, it might even be more important if you don't like the person you are in contact with. Even if you happen to just flat out hate your boss, it's completely acceptable for him to visit you in your office without a direct invitation. However, if you walk into your boss's office and have a seat without a direct invitation, you could be facing some pretty intense conversations about what is appropriate.

Then again, it is also the same with a teenager's bedroom, but who is in control of that relationship?

What about the situation?

What type of social situation is are you in that you are trying to determine the appropriate personal space? Is it a cocktail party with some of your best friends? Is it a pitch meeting in the boardroom? A fishing trip with your father in law? A public lecture?

In each of these situations, you'll have to act different and keep different amounts of space. That is the case even if all of the people are the same.

For example, while you will keep a great deal of distance in the board room or during a meeting, you might feel more comfortable getting closer during a cocktail party, even if it is just to hear someone. At a public lecture, you might feel okay being close to someone because the seats are close, but on a subway with plenty of open seating, it is different. It all has to do with common decency and the situation – and each situation is different.

Age

You might think that age has nothing to do with it, and it might not for some people. It's most relevant when talking about children, young adults, and teenagers. Children are much more open and naïve to other people than adults are, because they are either too innocent to know the problems, or because they themselves break social boundaries all the time. This is why kids are more likely to run and jump on someone when they see them, not thinking that the person could have a personal bubble.

Age is also important as you get older too. If you meet someone at a bar, a 32 year old man can get closer than a 65 year old man could to a 30 year old woman.

Purpose & Personality

One of the hardest parts of personal space to determine is just how much the person's personality has to go into personal space.

If you put aside every other quality that determines personal space, the most important is personal preference. You can tell a lot about someone's need for personal space by reading someone's attitude, mood, intention or relation to you. While someone may like a lot of personal space one day, the next she might want someone who is a little closer. Sometimes people will ask for you to move away or ask for you to be closer. If you are comfortable being closer to that person, than get closer. If you aren't, then tell them you aren't comfortable. However, there is no debate if a person tells you to move away.

Don't always assume that someone doesn't like you just because they want you to stand further away from them – you don't always know what makes a person tick or what annoys someone about a person. The world doesn't revolve around your thoughts and feelings, after all.

Sometimes someone will step away from you, and they might mean nothing by it at all, it is just a simple shifting of weight. Still, you have to respect that that person wanted to move away. Do not be a jerk and take a step towards them or make some kind of rude noise about the movement.

Sometimes, those wanting to have their own little bubble do have a specific reason why they don't want you near them.

Some people, for example, invade personal space on purpose – both to intimidate them and consequently manipulate them. While that might not be you, they might think that it is. Or maybe they just don't like you – that is a fact of life that we all have to live with, not everyone is going to like us all the time.

Other people try to use this tactic to further advance a relationship into a more intimate level, ironically, this very thing can cause the opposite reaction. Sometimes, someone will move away because they want you to chase them. This is usually only done in a romantic relationship where BOTH parties agree that it is a relationship. Don't believe that someone is playing hard to get unless you know for 100% fact that they are playing hard to get.

Again: do not assume someone is playing hard to get if they move away. You have to know that they are playing hard to get in order to appropriately invade their personal bubble.

When it comes to personality, extroverted people naturally tend to keep less distance than introverts. This is because they are getting their energy from those people, where introverts get their energy from themselves. It has nothing to do with how they appear on the outside. Even if you know someone's personality type, that doesn't mean you can just crowd the extroverts.

As you can tell, a lot of body language is just how well you can read other people, and that is never more obvious than when it comes to personal space.

Using Personal Space to Your Advantage

Personal space doesn't have to be something that hurts you or is something you need to work around. Instead, it is something that you can use to your advantage.

But first, you should know how to tell someone that they are in your personal space. Knowing when you are uncomfortable and how to react will help you understand how someone else is feeling, and will give you greater insight into how to use personal space.

Of course, you can simply take a step back or move away, but sometimes that isn't enough if a person is a chronic offender. You can always say, "I'd like a little breathing room," or "I think you are standing too close," but that doesn't always give the best impression. Many people use their nonverbal, body language skills because it doesn't seem as rude.

Something that you shouldn't try to do is fight fire with fire. You are likely to just make someone more hostile and cause a bigger problem. Think about two chicken trying to fight: they both totter around with their chests puffed up until one of them makes a move. In the end, no one really wins and they both end up hurt.

So since most of our meetings are supposed to be in a productive and peaceful context, we need to treat space invasion in a more subtle and elegant ways.

So how can you tell someone to back up?

The first thing you should try to do is change how you feel about it. Can the person realistically step away? No, standing back to back with someone on the subway in July isn't the most comfortable thing, but when the cars are packed, sometimes you don't really have any other options. If it is in business or a more spacious area, you have some choices to make.

If the reason is a cultural one or a status related, consider if that's worth resisting it, since it's an honest mistake. Is it really worth offending someone else because you are a little uncomfortable? But know that if this is in a personal situation, like at a bar or at a party, you should absolutely say something.

If you do tell someone that they are invading your personal space and they do not stop, the best thing you can do is try to leave. Removing yourself from the situation is giving you the most space you can get, and that will make everyone feel better. If you cannot get away, just try to move away slowly or find someone that you can trust and wouldn't mind being close to.

Another option to consider when someone is near you, especially in a business situation, is that this invasion is done on purpose: as an attempt to intimidate you or, on the opposite, to try getting closer to you to warm up the relations between you – many people don't realize (but you now will) that they are probably doing the opposite of warming you up.

The Best Steps to Take to Get More Space

Instinctively, the first move you'll probably make is to step back and into an open space. You need to retain your space, so you naturally move backwards, seeking out either someone who can comfort you or an open space where you can breathe. If your company observant enough or if they don't have an ulterior motive, they will notice it and hopefully respect that and not try to move forward. However, if they aren't as observant, they will try to step into that space, maybe seeking out a little more room for their own personal space. Men will often do this.

 If they're not observant or still want to be in your personal space, this little bit of movement can occur several times throughout your conversation or during the time you are together. You might find yourself moving several feet before your time is over – and that should be an obvious sign for the other person, especially in retrospect. If the specific relationship is important enough to you or if it is with someone who is your superior, and you need something from the other party, it may be worth to "suffer" their comfortable personal distance. Once again, this is just standing or "safe" touching – anything that makes you genuinely uncomfortable or touching that isn't appropriate needs to be dealt with in a different way.

Make a Barrier

If, on the other hand, you decide to stay where you are (in cases where there is nowhere to move), you should be on guard and to keep away the invader you can create a barrier. To make a barrier, either to find an actual barrier like a table, or to fold your arms. Do not use something like a purse, as some thieves will use that to get exactly what they want: your money.

It will make you feel more secure and will deter the other party from getting closer. Sometimes it can be as simple as just not responding to them, especially if they are talking. It might seem difficult, but it can be the safest route to take.

If all that fails, you still have one option left - get even closer to that person and see who wins in an awkward off. Take the initiative and invade their space too, and see if they don't back up. It may feel very awkward, now that you stand even closer, but it shows that you're not intimidated and in control. This will work best if the person has a lot of space behind them, but you don't have any space near you to move into.

The Other Way Around

What if you're the intruder or the person encroaching on someone else's space? If you are noticing it, then it is probably a problem for the other person as well.

If you have taken a step and then noticed a change in the tone or direction of the conversation or just the between the two of you – as in it has changed to a more hostile or defensive one, take a casual step back and continue the conversation from that distance.

If it is really bad, say, "Sorry," and take a step back. That will allow you to acknowledge that it was a problem and move on quickly.

Can I Use Space Invasion to my Benefit?

You can absolutely se space invasion to your benefit, but it can also backfire and cause you many problems than some of the other options that you have tried.

Invading another person's space, no matter who that person is to you, can be an effective tactic to confuse them, overpower them, or manipulate them to do your will or take your advice. But it is still a very risky tactic, even if you know the person, because you can't be 100% sure about how they will react, especially if you haven't done something like that before. Some people may seem like they are easy targets to manipulate or dominate, but the can burst when put under this kind of pressure. Remember that you don't always know someone's history, and they may have something traumatic that makes them very, very uncomfortable with another person. So unless you truly believe it's better to get close to them, for whatever reason, you might want to try some other tactic.

What about flirting?

Is getting into someone's personal space helpful in flirting or to warm up relationships? Again, it's a risky move that should be used with intense caution, but for some people it might just work.

The question you have to ask yourself is this: is the person you're trying to get is into you at all? Will they feel comfortable if you try to get close to them? If you're on a date and everything goes well, then you should try to get closer or use touch. If it is met with any kind of resistance (i.e. recoiling, frowning, or standing back with bewildered expression on their face), immediately step back. If they don't do any other those, it's a great sign that your date is comfortable with you. Take into consideration that it's a process; it doesn't mean that if they recoil back they don't like you, it can simply mean that you're not there yet. Still, do not do ANYTHING to make a person feel uncomfortable.

Now what?

There is a lot that goes into personal space: from the amount of room that a person needs, which varies per person, to the amount of space that a person would like – those are often very different numbers. The size of that necessary bubble is affected by many factors that we don't always think about, but probably should: culture, habits, socio-political status, and even gender.

The invasion of that bubble is frowned upon in our social interactions, especially between opposite genders, and should be generally avoided unless you try some sort of business tactic that you know will work. Space invasion causes us to be very aware of ourselves, our habits, and our actions. That means that it can be a very uncomfortable experience that gets more and more uncomfortable. That can ruin your relationship with a person, no matter what the relationships is, for a long, long time.

Chapter 8:
Sitting Body Language

So much of our study of body language focuses on standing, the face, and touch. However, when we are sitting, we tend to do things differently than we do when we stand up. In fact, we actually get more information from seating positions than we do when someone is standing, because we hold a lot of our emotions in our leg placement. When you sit, your legs don't do anything, which means that they become something that we can move and adjust easily – much like we do with our hands or face when we are standing. This comes in handy when you are at a business meeting or sitting at a dinner date with someone.

When sitting, your legs have nothing else to do but to give out great nonverbal information.

But what exactly are your legs saying?

Indications of Interest

The first group of leg positions when a person is sitting that you should know about are the indications of interest. You want to make sure to notice where the "points" of the leg, the foot and the knees, are pointing during the discussion. In sitting scenarios, where the main part of a person's leg is pointing is where the attention is.

Think about it: if you are sitting with someone and you are giving them your complete, full attention, you are probably going to have both knees and your feet pointed toward that person.

Another form of orienting when seated comes in the shape of the knee point - when one leg is folded under the other and the knee marks the direction of attention. Some people feel more comfortable when they are sitting with their legs folded. If that happens, it isn't a sign of them being uninterested, but rather a sign that they feel comfortable having you around. They don't feel like they will have to get to their feet anytime soon.

The important thing is that however the person is sitting, most of their attention (at least 75%) is directed straight towards you!

Men – Spread Legs

When we talk about sexual interest, men tend to be far more open and willing to show their interest than women are. They do something called "displaying the crotch" or sitting with their legs spread wide apart. Some women calls this "man spreading." It might be done to show availability or to show virility.

Men who sit like this are usually signaling, though they often don't realize it, that they feel dominant, strong and even a little smug - this position takes a lot of space (which has been a big problem on mass transit and theaters) and exposes their groin for the whole world to see.

Needless to say, especially depending on the man's choice or attire or the position of his hips, it can be really easily to offend others, or on the contrary it can also attract someone. So while spreading them wide for everyone to see is a good way to show confidence, if you don't want to annoy anyone - mind the distance between your knees.

Women - Shoe play

Women love shoes, and there is no doubt that they put on their best shoes when they want to show someone that they are attracted to them. Females have something a bit more sophisticated than spreading their legs – though some of them still do that: they play with their shoes when they want to attract attention.

This can manifest in a few different ways: the shoe dangling off their foot, they remove and enter their foot back and forth into it. Such display can drive men crazy, because it reminds them of the repeated action during intercourse. Women will also point the foot, making it look even longer than it already does because of the heel.

Sitting Cross Legged (Leg over Leg)

Crossing one leg over the other, for both men and women) is one of the most popular ways of sitting, and has many variations that mean almost the same thing. Women, for example, prefer the tight leg cross to emphasize their legs features. Men often cross the ankle of one leg over the knee of their other leg, but they sometimes sit tight legged as well.

The leg over leg or crossed position is usually done with the dominant leg on top, especially if that leg on top is bouncing or moving. While crossing the legs may indicate, for some people, a closed off or a reserved attitude, it's not always so. That type of sitting has a lot to do with beauty, habit, and comfort. Women thinks it looks attractive, and it is one of the best ways to make a chair more comfortable for a person, especially in a crowded space as it actually brings the hips in and makes them smaller. You will see a woman do this if she feels like her personal bubble has been invaded.

Women have more trouble than man sitting in uncrossed positions mainly because their clothing often doesn't allow that (mini-skirts) or because it's an established habit.

Leg Stretch

Sometimes it isn't about the way a person sits, but the way that person gets into that position. A very sexual display with the legs females utilize extremely effectively is the leg stretch that gets them into any sort of position. Some women will do it before they get up to get even more attention.

Women can easily use this flirting gesture to draw attention, especially if she's crossing and uncrossing them frequently – if you've seen the movie *Basic Instinct*, it is likely engrained in your mind.

Both Feet on the Ground

Placing both feet on the ground is the natural position that many of us sit in. However, the placement of hands during this position tells you a lot. Women will put their hands on their knees or play with their clothing if they are feeling uncomfortable. Men will often bounce one of their legs.

If a woman feels comfortable, they will often start doing something else, while a man will slouch back and maybe clasp his hands behind his head.

Tension:

Men and women can also show tension with how they sit. Here are the ones you need to be on the lookout for if someone is uncomfortable or tense:

Locking Ankles

Locking of the ankles is a way to show that someone is restraining themselves. It is a motion that is similar to biting the lip, holding oneself from slipping another word. It can hide emotions of anger, frustration, fear or other negative emotion.

Men will lock their ankles beneath the chair or wrap both legs around the legs of the chair itself. Usually their hands will form fists. Women will usually close both legs and turn them to the side while their hands rest on their knees or to their side.

Keeping the knees together

This one is a tricky one to interpret, especially because it really depends on the person. Many people interpret someone as reserved or timid if they sit with their knees together, but many people sit that way because it is socially acceptable. Women sit with their knees together so that no one can look up their skirts. On the contrary, men have no excuse for using such display - and it's quite rare to observe such an obvious display of insecurity.

Feeling at Home

In informal relaxed circumstances, a lot of how someone positions their legs will depend upon everything from how much space there is, the size of the person, and the clothing that a person is wearing. In casual situations, there isn't any way to sit that is more proper than any other way. Most informal positions have the tendency to be spread out and take strange forms: think about how you look while you are sitting on the couch watching television.

Placing the feet on an ottoman, table, or another part of the sofa or chair is the ultimate "I'm comfortable" single. If you see that, the person does not view you as a threat whatsoever.

Chapter 9:
The Use of Body Language

When we have discussed that the nonverbal canvas of the language is so wide and gigantic, we must admit its usability. Body language is both conscious and unconscious work of the human body. Many people reveal that they use effective body language without knowing that they are actually using the body language. When it comes to the delivery of messages and effective means of making this action a real success, the supreme triumph relies on the most active use of body language.

Many people can never communicate in public gatherings effectively because they lack the appropriate and necessary skills for polishing their body gestures and resulting implicit language. All you need is to make yourself efficient in the use of this reliable mode of communication. Although there are by no means rule of thumbs accessible for implicit language and its use, yet there are many things which can guide the way towards use of successful body language.

Body language is a wide area of study but here we will be discussing some master points for the use of body language:

One posture can help you gain uncountable power:

If we start reviewing the literature on body language, there will be copiousness of suggestions on power postures. Many of you can feel the unrest while attending a huge audience, or while conveying your message to some respectable audience. The major reason is the uneven body language. Power postures refer to a firm body pose which can serve as the body, major hub of power. It adds the maximum strength to the body and as a result the speaker can convey the message with utmost zeal and strength.

Now the power postures do not have any universal rule. For each person the power posture varies. Some people are comfortable in attaining the power through stiff bodies; others feel gigantic confidence when they have lean body postures.

Power postures are extremely effective if there is direct contact between the audience and the speaker. Direct contact refers to the absence of any physical fence. Like dice or rostrum. When there is not anything to hide behind, you have to be extra cautious, so try crafting your individual power pose. None other than you can craft the best and most efficient power posture.

Smile can turn the tables:

Whether it is some negotiation table or some issue under the discussion, the participants can change the whole story by a simple movement of lips. When we ponder upon the body language, only the smallest body part, which we entitle lips, can play the chief function. The linguistic experts say that nonverbal communication is highly driven by smiles and lip movements.

When you are addressing a large audience you cannot give flat or even expressions. The expressions on your face must be accompanied by frequent smiles and facial expressions. When you are not smiling during the entire conversation, it states and depicts that the confidence level is shattering or absent anywhere. When during an unsympathetic talk among the corporate executives, one of the participants extends mild smile, the whole table can revolve along the pleasant discussion.

Hand movements matter a lot:

Now talking about body language how can we forget about the hands? When having a harsh debate you may have seen people using hands so brutally that the message seems very rude and uncomfortable. However, the hand movements have full potential to convey the message in a convincing manner. If we start pondering upon the use of hands in our day to day communication and conversation, we can easily witness the clarity and precision of our message delivery.

Hand movements vary from people to people, but it is valid fact that hand movements can convey much of the information without any use of spoken words. Nevertheless there is a minor difference flanked by the effective and ineffective use of hand movements. Excessive use can establish a bad reputation. Some experts suggest that if you have the natural tendency to use hand movements you can use it as a competitive advantage for you communicating and speaking skills. If you owe the blessing of the knowledge about the use of hands, as a tool of body language, you will eventually reach the destination of constructive public speaking.

When you study the brain imaging details you can see that there is a certain portion of the human brain, which is more responsive to the visual signals, so using hands as affirmative action can make your audience more interested in your message. You may not need to quantify your suggestions; all will be done by your hands. Make perfect trial for this important body language aspect.

Practice through mirror expressions

If you have encountered a situation in which you will be handling the audience for the first time you may entail a number of different fears and frights. But every man had his first step for the first time somewhere in the life. So never quit because if your undue fears and unnoticed weaknesses.

The first step to getting into the world of body language and communication is to make you equipped with the necessary confidence. The foremost thing is to make you easy at talking. Body language can be an abundant power booster. So mirror practice is highly needed. Make yourself normal and natural in front of a mirror. Keep a strict eye on all kinds of your body movements and procedures. You may not be an expert on the initial encounter with the mirror yet you can easily play a good game with mirror practice. Never forgo your weaknesses. All you need is to behave like as if you are standing in front of the real audience. Feel free to behave naturally and within your periphery. In this way you can easily notice your strength. Problems, if any, can easily be fixed on the spot. So make mirror your friend. Be natural in front of your friend, and dig out all your weaknesses as well as the strong areas in the field of public speaking.

Situations that call for the analysis of body language

People who have already known the benefits of analyzing body language are now using it for their own gain so as not to make mistakes in various situations. The main areas where body language analysis is being used a lot these days include both professional and personal situations:

Professional situations

1. Job interviews

Interviewers focus mainly on body language so as to know if the interviewee is suitable for a certain job opening or not.

During job interviews, a lot of questions are asked. The main focus by interviewers is not on the answers that the interviewee is giving but in the manner in which he is presenting himself as he answers the questions.

An interviewer can for instance tell if you are comfortable with the questions being asked or not and he can continue to change the questions according to his analysis.

An interviewer can also tell if the interviewee is confident or not and this determines the outcome of the interview. If you are confident, it means that you are capable and ready to take up the new job and new responsibilities. This is in fact one of the most important things that interviewers check out for during interviews.

If an interviewee's body language appears uncomfortable or out of control, it can mean to the interviewers that he was not well prepared and so he may not be ready for the job. Interviewees are always required to research the company and be ready for some of the common questions that are asked during interviews. If he is ill prepared, he loses his chance of getting a job and this will easily reflect through his body language.

Both interviewers and interviewees have their part to play in this. If you are going for an interview, know that what you say will not matter as much as how you say it. Interviewers know very well how to watch your body language and will give you a job or deny you the chance depending on your body language. You therefore have to portray the best behavior.

As an interviewer, always be on the lookout for the body language so as to determine if you have the right candidate or not. You can tell a lot about a person through their body language. You can for instance tell if they are ready to work, if they are organized, confident, trustworthy, and truthful among other important aspects.

2. Criminal investigations

This is another professional situation that calls for body language analysis. On many occasions, the accused do not tell the truth as it is and so, the investigator has to watch how they are saying it so as to know if they are telling the truth or not. This can be used to determine whether a person has actually committed a crime or not.

An investigator watches the body language and if the accused clear their throat first before answering a question, this may mean that they are buying time in order to think of what to say. This is a sure way to know that they are not telling the truth.

If the accused does not maintain eye contact, it means that they are not telling the whole truth and that they fear that the investigator will find the truth through their eyes, which are believed to be the windows to one's soul.

Stammering is also an indication that the accused is lying, as well as changing the pitch of their voice during the interview. If he goes silent, in most cases it means an admission of wrong doing.

Fidgeting, moving one's feet, raising one's shoulders, looking away and blushing are some indications that the accused is not comfortable with the questions being asked by the investigator.

An expert investigator that knows so much about body language can easily tell when the truth is being said or not. He will know what kinds of questions to ask depending on how the accused is responding.

Personal situations

Body language can be used be a person to create lasting relationships. There are so many instances in your personal life you will use body language analysis in order to determine whether you are in the right relationship or not.

You can for instance spot a liar by the way they behave when they are with you, and this will tell you if a person is the right one to be friends with or not. If someone is constantly lying, it means that you are in the wrong relationship.

Someone in a relationship does not have to keep talking about their feelings. As they say, actions speak louder than words and so, body language can be used as a way to determine one's feelings. A hug, for instance, means that someone really likes you. Someone who gets close to you when you are talking is one that is interested to hear what you have to say. This is the kind of friend you can confide in.

When talking to a friend or a loved one, their body language can determine if they are actually paying attention to what you are saying or not. This will communicate a lot of things to you, either they do not like you, they do not like what you are saying, or they are troubled. With such discernment, you can know what to do in order to strengthen your relationship. If the person leans back when you are talking, it is an indication that they are not interested in what you are saying, or they feel superior to you.

When you listen to someone, ensure that you maintain eye contact. Otherwise you will not be paying attention to what they are saying. The other person may feel that you are only waiting for your chance to speak and when that comes, he may not pay attention to you as well. This is one killer of relationships as it is an indication of selfishness on the part of people who are supposed to be friends.

People enter into relationships for different reasons. It is up to you to determine the kinds of relationships you have, if they are healthy or not, and body language can help you so much with this.

Chapter 10:
Types of body language

Body language can make you one step ahead in the field of communication and message delivery. Nonverbal communication is significant not only in personal communication but also in formal corporate settings. When it comes to informal discussions, the rounds are wider and more diverse, as this communication will vary from one relation to another. As informal communication is prone to human emotions and relations, so it is a diverse area of discussion. On the grounds of formal and corporate discussions, one has to be extremely alert and watchful regarding this category of communication.

Major categories of Body language:

Body language is frequently categorized into following major subcategories:

> Parts of the body

> Intent

Parts of the body

As far as the nonverbal communication is concerned, all of the body parts of the human body play a vital role in making the communication better and more effective. Here is the discussion of major body parts involved in the nonverbal communication and implicit discussions:

> **The Head** –it composes the major visual posture of the human body while talking or meeting anyone. The

whole skull along with other parts can make the communication more result oriented. While delivering your message the movement of the head makes the message clear, an effective nodding or shaking can change the whole story. All the movements horizontally as well as vertically are crucial. When talking to any one keeping the head movements irregular a make the communication boring and ineffective.

> **Facial Expressions**–Implicit communication is best understood by means of facial expressions. Along with its diverse number of muscles, the face makes the feelings and emotions clearer and message oriented. While using different facial expressions one can communicate a diverse number of feelings and different states of mind. From anger to love, the facial expression holds the capacity to communicate everything. So one must have the impending to make the message entirely successful using this natural mode of communication. While using facial expression, the understanding of the decoder is also very crucial.

> **Eyebrows** –The movement and flexibility of eyebrows an make your body language more effective and meaning oriented. Frowning can be worn to suggest an apparent message. Similarly, the up and down movement of eyebrows has clear meanings and messages. So while using body language, you must keep a strict eye on the use of eyebrow movements.

> **Eyes**–Eyes are a clear depiction of one's emotions and behaviors. So as far as the body language is concerned eyes have the most effective result of making the message more understandable.

- > **Nose** –The nose is also effective for nonverbal communication like the nostrils flaring can depict the clear message of anger.

- > **Lips**–A number of different messages can be conveyed using lips. It can be variable like puckered, snarling, smiling, opened, kissing closed, tight.

- > **Tongue**–Although it may not be used in formal or corporate discussion, yet it is highly usable in non-formal communication. Different tongue postures embrace, thrashing of lips, in, rolled out, tip up or down.

- > **Jaw** - lower jaw left or right, clinched, open or closed

- > **Body Posture**–Using all the body parts, the placement of different body parts, their movement and placement make a definite body posture used for delivering a perfect implicit message.

- > **Body proximity**–It refers to a particular distance maintained by the speaker while communicating a specific message. The distance can be very small in the case of informal discussions.

- > **Shoulder movements**–The shoulders and their movements can add energy to the message. Different shoulder positions can result into different messages like hunched or hanging.

- > **Arm placement**–Make your arms effective in the delivery of the message. Arms can be placed like crossed placement or straight placement.

- ➢ **Legs and feet placement**–Not only the movement of the legs and feet is vital, but their placement with reference to the communication partner is also imperative. In addition, the sagging shoes conveys specific emotions and messages. .

- ➢ **Hand and finger gestures**–Some people irregularly play with their own fingers while communicating, while others use hands to make their message more clear and affirmative. .

- ➢ **Handling and placement of objects**- Although you may ask about the relevance of these objects with reference to body language, yet how you use communication aids like pen and papers, is very significant in making the message more effective.

The intent of using the body language

One more technique to cluster types of body language is using the basis of the Intent:

Intentional or Voluntary movements–All the body movements which are intentional and dealt with voluntary actions are termed as gestures. It includes eye blinking, thumbs up, down, finger movement and shaking the hands.

Involuntary movements– Apart from intentional movements, there are many movements which are beyond one's control. This category also signifies the reflexive actions. Some linguistic experts say that sweat patterns are also a part of this involuntary category of actions. Any body movement you have no control over falls in this class.

Voice control

While the voice is not a part of nonverbal communication, yet its different features and characteristics play a vital role in giving an implicit meaning to the communication.

While usually seen as body language, quality of voice and modulation are a split group from body language. Many different elements of voice are needed to be discussed like the pitch of the voice. If the pitch of voice is too low, it usually depicts a lack of confidence. The high pitch can result in a number of connotations. Sometimes high pitch is needed to make the voice audible for everyone around. Moreover, loudness also entails a number of variable meanings and connotations. Breathing patterns are also referred to as the significant and vital characteristic of nonverbal communication. If breathing is not in the control of the speaker, it can easily shatter the whole message.

Chapter 11:
Message Clusters Delivered Through Body Language

Body language constitutes more than 50% of what we are communicating and so, it forms an integral part of our communication. For effective communication, it is important for one to know what they can say and what they cannot say through their body.

Body language is categorized into message clusters of postures and signals depending on the emotions and the mental states of the person communicating. Dealing with these clusters is much easier when one is learning body language than dealing with one element at a time. It is also more accurate to interpret body language in these clusters.

a) The Aggressive Body Language Cluster

This is body language that is an indication of physical threat. It is used more as it is better than engaging in a physical fight even for the most powerful people. Many people know that fighting can be hurtful even when you are the strong one, and also, it is socially unacceptable. In its place, they use their body to communicate their deeper feelings.

Most aggressive feelings can be shown on the face and some of the signs to check out for are:

- ➢ Sneers

- ➢ Pulsed lips

- ➢ A disapproving frowning face

➢ Full snarls

➢ The eyes can stare and hold the gaze for a long time, and the person can also squint

Physical attacking signals can also be used to show signs of aggression in a person. The person may clench their fists, for instance, to show that they are ready for a fight. A red face is also an indication signal.

Invading another person's space is also a show of aggression. This can be shown by approaching a person, touching them and even going to places you are sure they will be without an invitation.

Aggression may also be in the form of insulting gestures. Arm thrusts and chin tilts are some of the gestures that could stir up anger in another person.

If a person bangs a door or table or throws something away, it is a way to show just how angry they are. These gestures accompanied by the facial gestures and words can easily tell you how angry the other person is.

b) The Attentive Body Language Cluster

This is basically a show of interest when you are talking to another person, or you are following what the other person is doing. The attentive body language shows deep and real interest in the other person, and it can be interpreted as a call for reciprocation.

➢ An attentive person is definitely listening keenly.

➢ They will ignore all forms of distractions to show just how attentive they are.

➢ If the person is still, it means that they have ignored everything else just to listen to what is being said.

➢ Another sign of deep attention is when one leans forward to the person who is talking.

➢ An attentive person will also tilt their heads to the side.

➢ They gaze at the other person without looking away.

For an attentive person wanting to know more, check out for the following:

➢ Patience

➢ An open body

➢ A slow nod

➢ Interest noises like uh, mm, oh, huh

➢ Use of reflections

c) Bored Body Language Cluster

The entire body of a bored person will show. This is a much easier signal to read even without looking for other cues. If you are trying to persuade such a person, it is better to try it another time because you will bore then further. The language of boredom is interpreted from:

➢ Distraction: A person is constantly looking away and everywhere else except where the person talking is.

➢ Repetition of the same actions like drumming fingers

> Tiredness. They may show this by yawning, slouching down on their seats, leaning against a wall or sagging from where they are standing.

> Facially, the person looks blank and with no interest at all

d) Confident Body Language Cluster

Some people appear confident and sure of themselves while others seem anxious and unsure. These are feelings that are hard to hide so if you are looking for confidence in a person, you will easily see it through their body language.

Some of the cues to check out for are:

> Stillness: Anxious people are generally tense. Their bodies are in constant motion. It is very easy to spot this out. A confident person, on the other hand, can be able to stand in one position for a long time but an anxious person always gets happy feet when standing, and they keep moving from one place to the other.

A confident person will sit comfortably, leaning back in his chair while an anxious person will not even sit still. They lean forward and keep shifting on their chair.

Confident people will be able to hold their head still, but an anxious person will always be on the lookout for threats.

A confident person has total control of his hands when speaking, but an anxious person can even hold his hands together.

- Unhurried: Anxious people are always in a hurry, talking fast and moving their bodies very quickly. Confident people are not in a hurry at all. When talking, a confident person will go slower, adding pauses between his sentences and allowing people time to digest what he has just said. A moment of silence will be okay for a confident person and they can stay silent for as long as it is required, without feeling threatened.

- Uncovered: Confident people do not try to cover themselves with their hands, as anxious people do. They are open when communicating with other people. An anxious person will use defensive and closed body language, unlike a confident person.

  Confident people find it easy to communicate their feelings to other people without overdoing it. They can easily use their bodies to show just how they feel.

  Confident people appear natural. They do not seem as if they want to manage their bodies or their appearance. They are comfortable with the way they look, and so they can move around without worrying that someone is looking at them.

- Direct: Confident people are direct; they do not show that they are uncomfortable and that they could take off any minute.

  They take the time to greet people, smile at them and shake their hands with no hurry.

  They face people who are talking to them, and they are attentive to what the other person is saying. Anxious people will always look away to check out for any threats to the environment.

Confident people will wait for their turn to talk while an anxious person will always see the need to talk.

Confidence is a show of no fear; they do not feel threatened by any person or situation.

e) Defensive Body Language Cluster

When a person feels threatened, they exhibit defensive body postures. The most basic defensive body language is exhibited on the assumption that the other person will attack. Therefore the person tries to hide some vital body parts and their vulnerable points. Most people hold their hands across the chest or face as these are the likely parts that they will be hit, even when it is highly unlikely.

Other people fend off to defend themselves even when the other person is not attacking them. Sometimes the use of barriers is noticed; some people reduce themselves without knowing so as to defend themselves from a likely attack.

Another defense mechanism is rigidity, where muscles harden up so as to withstand the attack. Other people will walk to a safer place possibly to hide from the possible threat. All these are done without the person's conscious knowledge, but other people can easily know what he is trying to communicate.

To defend themselves, some people will look away just to avoid the attack and others will try to strike first. This happens so fast that the person exhibiting these body language movements is not able to think before acting.

f) Emotional Body Language Cluster

Emotions are best detected through nonverbal cues. The cues are general indicators and not certain guarantees; you have to watch out for other cues and to listen to the other person to know for sure that the cues they are exhibiting are really what you think they are.

Some of the cues, in this case, are:

Anger: This occurs when one is unable to achieve his goals. The signs are:

➢ Neck or face turns red or looks flushed.

➢ Snarling and baring of teeth.

➢ Some/all of the aggressive body language cues discussed above.

➢ Clenched fists.

➢ A show of power through body language.

➢ Invasion of body space through leaning forward to the other person.

Anxiety, nervousness and fear: this occurs when basic needs are threatened. Cues to watch out for here are:

➢ A pale face

➢ Cold sweat

➢ Dry mouth and/or trembling lips

➢ Damp eyes

- ➢ Speech errors

- ➢ Voice tremors

- ➢ Varying voice pitch

- ➢ Sweating

- ➢ Muscle tensions

- ➢ Fidgeting

- ➢ Gasping and trying to hold breath

- ➢ Defensive body language for instance crossing of arms and legs

Embarrassment: Transgression of values or guilty may cause frustration. This is shown through such cues as:

- ➢ A red or flushed face and neck

- ➢ Not able to look into other people's eyes

- ➢ False smiles, changing topic, grimacing

Sadness: This is an indication of depression. These cues can help you identify sadness in a person:

- ➢ Tears

- ➢ Drooping of the body

- ➢ Flat speech tone

- ➢ A trembling lip

Happiness: When goals and needs are met, the person will definitely be happy, and this can be shown through:

➢ Smiling even with the eyes

➢ An open body language

➢ A general relaxation of muscles

Surprise: When things occur unexpectedly, a person will be surprised and this is indicated by:

➢ Widened eyes

➢ Raised eyebrows

➢ Open mouth

➢ A sudden backward movement

Chapter 12:
Getting the Mastery of Body Language

If we signify that implicit language is covering half if our daily life contact, then it will not be counterfeited at the entire. There are a number of unspoken words and messages uttered in our daily life which are representative of our styles and cultures. Many people ask that if body language is innate within the human body, then what is the reason or paying concentration towards its mastery. The point of focus signifies that ne must be fully aware of all the strengths and weak points of one's body language. If we start exercising frequent concentration over our body language, we can reach the destination of the most effective communication.

The successful communication is a whole cyclic procedure. It entails that all the subjects implicated in the cyclic process are aware of the purpose and the notion of communication. The listeners, as well as the speaker, both are imperative for the complete success of communication. All these facts also connote for implicit nonverbal communication. The use of body language is complemented by smart and prompt understanding of all the gestures, postures, and positions. If the speaker is good at using variable gestures, even then the completion of process relies on the listener, which is the agent for decoding of the message and making the necessary adjustments, according to uttered message.

Now we will discuss the mastery of body language from two different perspectives:

As A Speaker:

If we talk about body language, the speaker has a lot of responsibility to deliver the clearest message with the utmost effort. Some of the major points which must be kept in mind by the speaker are as follows.

➢ While initiating the meeting or the conversation, the initial moves are very significant. Never take start with weak handshake. The handshake is the prior most encounters between the two parties, so it must be warm and full of energy. Encoding of nonverbal cues is the duty of the speaker. Encoding means that appropriate signal is given through the most accurate implicit body gestures so that the message is conveyed easily.

➢ Make your start extremely confident. The approach you loom an audience can help you catch the charisma of a perfect speaker. If you enter a meeting hall with shaky or gloomy posture, all of your impression can be put into the dark. So attempt to have a strapping and steady posture to convey that your confidence is large enough to complete the process of communication.

➢ Never divert your attention towards unimportant or irrelevant issues. Make the speaking activity fully alert and conscious. Some people start playing with their hairs or other body parts which state their lack of concentration. Whilst you are intriguing, all your body gestures and postures must be attentive and considerate.

➢ Make your voice a great support for your communication. The pitch, the frequency as well as the sound patterns has the capability to alter the message as well as the meaning of the whole conversation. If verbal communication is held by text and words, nonverbal is held with different characteristics of this voice.

➢ If you are starting a highly formal conversation or you are in a corporate gathering, all your body movements must be sophisticated and civilized. Do not engage in recreation with the items around lie pens, calendars or other objects placed on the table.

➢ Eye contact plays the pivotal role in making a fruitful conversation. So, whatsoever illustration or acoustic aid you are using for making the communication, never forget to maintain the eye contact. It is exceedingly swaying skill when you are having a large and scattered audience. Eye contact can illuminate a numeral of inherent ambiguities, in a way that the narrator is scattering self-belief all around.

➢ Make yourself presentable. It is not a part of the body, yet it is a way of couched communication. By picking the dress according to the gathering or occasion you actually portray that you are interested in the meeting and pay attention towards its peculiarities.

➢ Crossed arms are considered as a great peccadillo, in the sphere of implied gestures. While you are addressing the spectators, crossed arms depict that you are least bothered about all the formal prerequisites and his essentials. Make accurate arm location, depending upon the gathering and its size.

➢ The use of body parts and using the body language are two different perspectives. If a person is using the body parts for no reason. Like many people overly use hands while talking, this gives an overloaded impression of the conversation. If you want to be a perfect speaker all you need is to get equipped with effective body gestures. Not all conversation needs to be fully loaded with hand movements or eye gestures. If there is a light discussion with no formal arguments, then the voice tone needs not to be affirmative. If there is a large audience, which need to be persuaded for some strong belief, then hand movements may become crucial. All the visionary leaders in the history used to have tremendous body language which had a charismatic effect on the audience. Leadership personalities are always having one common trait, which is the exclusive persuasive ability.

➢ Always keep your presence prominent in the conversation session if you are a speaker. Many speakers lose the prominence and the eminence because they fail to become visible. If your body language is attractive and eye catching, listeners cannot keep themselves away from the speaker. Body language forms a whole ambiance around the speaker in a way that everything uttered by him is listening carefully. So make body language, your tool for becoming outstanding. The initial few minutes of the conversation are quite enough for forming the foundations for your discussion.

As A listener:

Mastery is not only required in uttering the implicit language and gestures, but it implies for the listener as well. As we mentioned that communication is a complete cyclic process, so it also calls for the attention of the listeners, or sometimes referred to as the decoder of the message.

> Be clear about the meanings and the inference of the message. If you are the spectator, you must watch out all the vital procedures involved in making the communication a perfect success. The know-how about the purpose of the communication can make it easy to understand the body language. Decoding the neural cues are the prerequisites for understanding the body language. If a marvelous speaker is in front of you and you are unable to decode his body language and gestures, then the communication channel is malfunctioning. So decoding is as significant as encoding. While we suggest developing the effective body language, we also recommended being excellent listeners who can catch the nonverbal cues within no time.

> The role of speakers becomes twofold if the there is a cross-cultural interaction. In this case, the listener must know about the clashes, ambiguities and mismatching of the body postures and gestures. In many circumstances, the spokesman desires to utter some optimistic note, but the listener, for the reason that, he lacks knowledge, takes it in a negative sense.

> If there is any kind of ambiguity, the speaker has the duty to make it clear that all the meanings understood and communicated are on the same grounds. In the event of cultural diversity, the speaker has the right that he can ask in advance but any ambiguities or clashes. If the listener takes it for granted the whole communication cycle will get disturbed and distorted. So the listener must also fulfill the whole responsibility.

➢ Posture is equally important for the listeners. While the communication process is undergoing, different body postures of the listeners can enhance the whole process and deliver a certain message to the speaker so that he can change , alter or modify his speaking. All this will result in clear communication.

➢ If you are attending some formal gathering, it is highly recommended that you carry out search regarding the topic and the speaker if already known. Searching for the speaker does not mean that you need to learn his profile. Reading about the speaker will let you know about his style, his frequently used gestures, and postures. In this way when you will reach at the real set, you will be eased by the prior knowledge about the speaker and his used body language. Many listeners lack the knowledge about the positions and the trick of judging the postures, so searching it in advance will surely help.

Body language is a diverse field of linguistics and anthropology. It not only varies from culture to culture, but it has great diversity along the individual personalities. These points have been discussed with a generalized approach, but cannot serve as the rule of thumb. You can enhance the use as well as the decoding of body language, after having a thorough set of exercise and practice.

Chapter 13:
Body Language Analysis in Serious Relationships

Serious relationships are quite tricky to create. Establishing a relationship based on trust only is not working as so many people are cheating in relationships, causing heartaches to their loved ones. If you are starting a relationship or you are already in the middle of a serious relationship, you no longer have to believe what you are told at all times in order to determine if you are in the right relationship or not. Check out his/her body language and you will know if for sure they are telling the truth or not.

Mastering the tricks in reading body language can help you at the beginning of a serious relationship and also as your relationship continues. This will save you in many situations that can be hurtful. Being able to pick out some of the clues he/she is sending your way can help you determine their personality as well as their feelings towards you.

Men's Body Language- What to Check Out

When a woman is looking to get involved with a man, she can have no better arsenal than the ability to be able to read what the man is saying, even when he has not said anything at all. A man's first approach will determine if he is actually a prince or he is out to have a good time. If he is looking for a short-term sexual relationship and nothing more, you will know through his:

➢ Cocky half smile

➢ Short stares

If he has an uneven grin, it means that he is a chameleon, not really sure of what he really wants. It will be a waste of time to get into a serious relationship with such a man.

Long stares for a man is an indication of sincerity and so, if you are looking for a boyfriend, this is the kind of man to get together with. Long stares means that he has nothing to hide. Many people who have something to hide will not give you a long direct stare because they are afraid that you could read behind their eyes, which is why this is an indication that he is a sincere guy with good intentions.

Some of the tell-tale signs that a man who is interested in you will exhibit are:

> Widening his eyes

> Fiddling his hair

> A need to draw your attention and gaze. This can either be by acting out a bit or moving away from his friends just so you may notice him.

If you are already in a relationship, you can easily tell if your partner is committed to you, his protectiveness and also about his emotional engagement through his body language. Watch out for slouched shoulders, an indication that you have really touched his heart. If he constantly gives you soft small kisses on the forehead or on the cheeks, it shows that he is really into you. A stroke of your hair is a sure sign that he is protective over you and that he will do anything for you. If these lack in your relationship, you now know where you are headed.

You can use body language analysis to know if your partner has sexual prowess too. Watch out for the strength and surety of his touch. A firm grip means that he has sex in his mind.

Licking of lips is also another indication that he is interested in a sexual relationship with you. If on the other hand a man does not touch you strongly or even get close, it means that he is not interested in a serious relationship with you. He may not be into a heart connection with you either. Men use their strength of touch to prepare a woman for the kind of relationship to expect thereafter.

A pinch on your bottom, something that offends so many women, is not a bad thing at all. It shows that your guy is confident with what you two have. This is a sexual way that many couples use in order to get each other's attention.

If you are already in a sexual relationship, you can tell the kind of man that you are dating easily through his body language during sex. A man who takes charge is confident about himself and will not hesitate to protect you when need arises. A man who gives you a chance to take over cares about your feelings. You can easily tell if a man is losing interest or not by the way he connects with you during intimacy. Always watch out for these signs so as to fix your relationship before things get out of hand.

Female Body Language- How to Read It

Women are mysterious and in some ways more complicated, so their body language is harder to read when compared to that of men. If a woman is into you, it will take a great deal of time for you to realize it. Women are not as obvious as men are, and they will try as much as possible to hide their intentions especially to the men that they like. However, you can still read a woman's body language if you are keen enough:

1. A woman's stance

This is one way through which you can tell what a woman is trying to communicate to you.

If she is standing with her hands crossed, it means that she is keeping you away, that she does not want to be approached. If on the other hand she is standing with her hands relaxed, facing you, it means that she is interested in a conversation with you. This is the best time to approach her.

If she has her back to you, this is not probably the best time to try conversing with her.

If a woman is seated and a part of her body is facing your direction, maybe her legs or her knees, it means that she could be interested in a conversation with you. If you are interested, you can approach her then.

2. A woman's face

A woman's face can communicate a lot of things without her need to talk to you.

If you look at a woman and you find her looking at you, this is an indication that she is interested in you. If she licks her lips or flutters at you with her eyelashes, it means that she is interested in you.

If you are trying to get her attention and she keeps avoiding eye contact with you, you may want to back off or to try another trick in order to get her attention.

If a woman gives you no eye contact during a conversation, there is no need to approach her at that moment because she is not into you at all.

3. Mannerisms she keeps repeating

If a woman constantly picks and plays with her hair, or fixes her hair every time you are with her, it is a sign of interest in you. If she does something over and over again when in her presence, it means that she is trying to win your attention and if you like her, this will be the time to talk to her.

Men are not quick to read a woman's body language, and sometimes they misinterpret it, causing a huge rift between two people who could form a great and lasting relationship. To avoid being misinterpreted, women try as much as possible to hide their intentions and feelings.

If she likes you:

> She will touch you and get close when talking to you.

> She will choose what to wear carefully when meeting up with you

> She will wear makeup when meeting up with you

> She will find an excuse just to see you, in your office, popular hangout or even in your house.

> She will ask for your help

> She will ask for your advice and opinion even in matters that do not concern you

> She wants to be in your company most of the time

> She invites you to her home, or out.

Body language is not really easy to interpret especially if you are doing it for the first time. If you continue observing other people closely, it can be easy to understand body language with time.

The good thing is that body language does not lie; you may lie with your words, but your body language will tell as it is. That is why this is the best way to determine if you are in the right relationship or not.

Chapter 14:
Effective Analysis of Body Language

Accept that reading body language is a hard task

People are different, and they express themselves differently. This is what makes understanding body language a complex affair. Interpreting what a personal is actually communicating will require more than just looking at what they are doing. You need to take the whole picture into perspective and analyze it in relation to their behavior and words. This way, you will know what they actually mean and if their words are the same as their body language.

If a person is anxious, it may not mean that they are having trouble at the office or at home or not; something else may be the problem. If they do not mention it to you, your interpretation may not be so clear until you hear what they have to say about it. That is why if you are not careful, you may end up misinterpreting someone's body language and not really understanding what they want to communicate.

Know that you could misinterpret body language

Many people misinterpret body language especially on the first day of observing another person. It is actually not easy to explain another person's feelings by just observing their behavior once, which is the reason you can easily misinterpret it. If you want to effectively understand a person's body language, you have to observe them on a few more occasions. Or listen to them as they talk. This way, it will be hard to make a mistake.

The problem with misinterpreting body language is that you may draw false conclusions about a person, and as you know, these conclusions could form the basis through which you see the other person.

An excited person, for instance, may run and hug you without thinking, and you may think that they are trying to send other signals other than their actual feelings.

Take all factors into consideration

To understand body language really well, take into consideration a person's personality, their verbal behavior, social factors as well as the general setting of the place they are in at that moment. All these are important for you to effectively understand their body language better. In the absence of some of these or all of these factors, it may be hard for you to understand the body language of people but if you observe them more than once, you can easily understand them better.

Interpreting body language should not be based on one observation

Looking at a person once is not enough to tell what they actually meant through their behavior. There are so many influences on our behavior, and one can behave differently in a similar situation the next time around. What you should do is to observe behavior the same way you watch TV; you have to watch an entire episode in order to understand a TV program well. The same way, you have to pay close attention to the person whose body language you want to interpret so as to really know what they are trying to communicate. A repetition of behavior by one person in similar situations will be easier to interpret, and you can accurately interpret it as compared to one's behavior once in one given situation.

Take your time so as to effectively understand people's behavior and personality through their body language.

Always consider individual differences

When it comes to body language, there is no similarity in the way people communicate. There is no standard basis that you will use in order to interpret different people's behaviors. Every person is different and so, in order to understand your person of interest's behavior, you have to pay close attention to them to understand better what they actually mean.

What is accurate for one person may not be accurate for another. For instance, there are people who will not maintain eye contact when lying but others will even gaze straight through your eyes trying to prove that they are not lying, yet they are lying. You have to be careful not to generalize body language from one person to the other because then you will be wrong in your analysis.

If someone is quiet, it may be because they do not want to admit a wrong doing yet they are guilty. Another person will be silent because they do not want to talk about that subject manner. People cry when they are happy, and others cry when they are sad. Understand the person better and you will be able to effectively interpret their nonverbal behavior.

Body language is different across culture

For some gestures, emotional expressions, and body language expressions, there could be major differences according to culture. Some cultures, for instance, will take eye contact to mean anger and resistance while others will mean approachability. When trying to interpret body language, understand these differences in culture so that you will do it successfully.

However, many gestures, emotion and body expressions are the same across cultures and so, it can be easy for you to interpret different body languages once you start paying attention. Again, it is important to understand a person better first and the environment they are in so that you will not be wrong in your interpretations.

Do not get in the way!

Some people are too obvious when they are watching others trying to understand them better. If the other person notices that you are closely watching them, they may inhibit a behavior that will give you the wrong ideas altogether. If you want to effectively interpret a person's body language, do not get in the way. Ensure that they are as comfortable as they could be and do not make it too obvious that you are watching them. Discretion is key. Give them some time to portray their behavior and to start communicating nonverbally, and then you can understand what they actually mean.

Know that body language is mainly about feelings

When trying to read body language, do not look for other interpretations other than a person's feelings. This is what they hide behind words and it slowly comes out in the way that they behave. If someone does not really like you, it will not be long before they show it however much they tell you that they like you. If someone is afraid of something, they do not have to tell you about it because it will come out automatically through their behavior. You can easily tell if one is just afraid or terrified about something and depending on what it is and the situation at hand, it may be easier for you to help them without them asking for your help.

Chapter 15:
Body Language Mistakes To Avoid

Body language is exhibited without the conscious knowledge of a person. That is why it is always used as the best way to identify a person's feelings. However, there are blunders one can make especially in a formal setting that could jeopardize their success. Once you are aware of such mistakes, it can be easier for you to avoid exhibiting them and they will save you from a situation. Some of these cues are:

a) **Slouching**: Many people interpret slouching as a show of disrespect. This is not the kind of signal you want to send out there especially in a professional setting. It is a show that you are bored, and you really want the other person to know about it. In a meeting, for instance, you could be communicating to your bosses that you do not want to be there and that you would rather be somewhere else. Try and maintain a good posture as a show of respect even when you are actually bored. This will promote engagement on both ends when you are in a conversation.

b) **Watching the clock**: It is a sign of impatience and disrespect if you keep glancing at the clock or your watch when you are talking to someone. It is also a sign of inflated ego. The interpretation, in this case, is that you have better things to do than talking to that person. It shows that you cannot wait to leave.

c) **Exaggerating gestures**: Use of exaggerated gestures shows just how much you want to insist on the truth. A confident person will use small and sure gestures when talking to other people. Controlling your gestures shows leadership and confidence. Use open gestures when you want to show that you have nothing to hide instead of using so many gestures to explain yourself. In most cases, people will think that you are not certain about what you are talking about.

d) **Scowling**: Having a grumpy face at all times is a way of shutting out other people around you. It shows that you are upset with people around you even if they have nothing to do with your bad mood. Many people are turned off by bad moods, and they may not get close to you. In a professional setting, this will not work out for you since you are required to work in a team on numerous occasions.

e) **Crossing your arms and legs to some extent**: These are open gestures that show your lack of interest in what the other person is saying. Even when other cues show that you are paying close attention to the person talking, he may get an idea that you are trying to shut him down or that you are not open to what he is saying. Sometimes folding one's hands feel comfortable, and people do it unconsciously without realizing the message they are passing across to the other person. You have to resist this urge if you want to have an effective communication with the other person.

f) **Exaggerated nodding**: This happens a lot but what the other person thinks is that you agree to something that you do not really understand. It could be a sign that you are showing an agreement to something that you actually do not agree with.

g) **Rolling eyes**: This is a show of total disrespect. It shows the other person that you do not really care about their position or status. Controlling this habit will be of great benefit to you.

h) **Inconsistency**: Your words should match your facial expressions otherwise people will get the idea that you are lying. Remember that body language does not lie. It will be hard for people to believe what you are telling them if you show something opposite through your body language. If for instance you show a smile nervously during a negotiation for an offer, the other person may feel that you are up to something and may not be willing to continue dealing with you.

i) **Fidgeting**: Not staying still shows that you are anxious. Some people fix their hair all through a conversation, and this shows the other person that you are anxious about something. Fidgeting is also a sign of distraction, and this may cut short the person talking as they will see that you are not following hat they are saying. In a professional setting, this will definitely ruin you.

j) **Weak handshakes**: A weak handshake shows that you lack confidence and authority. A super strong handshake is not good either as it can communicate aggression or a need to dominate on your part. Keep your handshakes firm at all times and you can adjust them according to the person you are greeting and situations.

k) **Avoiding eye contact**: Eye contact has been discussed in detail in this guide. It is very important if you do not want to send the wrong message to the other person. If you constantly avoid eye contact, it means that you have something to hide. This could arouse suspicion on the other end. It also shows that you lack confidence and that you are not interested in what the other person is trying to communicate. These are messages you do not want to send in a business setting.

l) **Clenched fists**: This communicates that you are an argumentative and very defensive person. Even when you do not mean it, other people will start to avoid you as these are traits people do not really like.

m) **An intense eye contact**: In as much as maintaining eye contact is good as it shows confidence, intelligence, strength and leadership, too much of it is not good as well. An intense gaze is a show of aggression or a need to dominate. Eye contact should not be held for too long, the way you break that contact matters too. If you suddenly look down, it is a show of submission. Looking on the side shows that you are confident.

n) **Turning away from people**: When you turn away from someone that is talking to you, or you do not lean forward to a conversation, it shows that you are not really paying attention or you are uninterested in what is being talked about. It can also show that you are uncomfortable and that you do not trust the person that is talking. If you want to show interest in a conversation, shift your focus and attention to them.

o) **Getting too close**: Getting too close to a person you are not really close to is an invasion of their personal space, and this means that you do not respect them or their personal space. This makes people around you quite uncomfortable.

Conclusion

In the end, I would like to be obliged for your efforts and resources spent on having a look at this manuscript, although this short summary may not be enough to make you skillful in nonverbal communication and the use of body language, yet I think that we have reached to the goal of providing the main information about this wide topic of body language.

We wish that all the interested readers can find this book as a guideline for adopting nonverbal communication. If you have never given a second thought to body language, it is the time to explore this distinguishing feature of the nonverbal statement.

Assorted aspects of body idiom along with its assortment and variety of techniques have been explained so that any confusion can be settled on the early stage and you can move on to the practical application of this fabulous mode of conversation.

We also wish that by reading this manuscript you can polish your innate skills of nonverbal communication and can conquer all types of communication platforms and all gatherings, whether public or private because body language is vital for communication.

If you enjoyed this book, please leave a review for this book on Amazon

Thank you and good luck!

Public Speaking

The art of getting attention and maintaining attentiveness

Table of Contents

Introduction   111

Chapter 1: Characteristics of a Good Public Speaker   112

Chapter 2: Look the Part   115

Chapter 3: How to Practice Public Speaking   119

Chapter 4: Tips for Public Speaking   124

Conclusion   127

Introduction

Public speaking is something that you will have to do at some point in your life whether it is for a school project, to accept an award, or in your job. It is something that most people do not like to do or which they are not all that comfortable with doing, but it is a part of life. If you are interested in becoming a better public speaker, either because you admire those who give great speeches or you work in a job that requires a lot of public speaking, this guidebook can help you. It is full of all the tips that you need to know in order to get started. You will learn the characteristics of a good public speaker, what you should wear to your speech, how to practice for the speech, and some other tips in order to get started. Use this guidebook to get on the right path to great public speaking today!

Chapter 1:
Characteristics of a Good Public Speaker

Public speaking is something that you are going to have to deal with for the rest of your life. You will have to give presentations of some sort for your whole educational life and even for some of the sports and other activities that you might be in. When you enter the workforce, you might have to do some public speaking in order to get a job, to talk to the client, or even to announce news on television. There are many different types of public speaking that are out there and there are many different situations where you might have to give a speech. Despite all of this, there are many people who find that it is difficult to give a public speech. They might be worried that they are going to look bad while they are doing it, that they will forget their lines, or they just do not like to talk in front of other people. Even if you have these fears, it is important to learn how to get over them so that you are able to perform in your role. This chapter is going to talk about some of the characteristics that come with being a good public speaker. This can help you to see if you have some of these characteristics already; if not, you will be able to develop these characteristics in order to make speech giving easier. Some of the characteristics that are present in a good public speaker include:

> ➢ Solid content—even if you do not have a natural charisma about you like some speakers do, you will be able to get the audience on your side simply by having content that is solid and valuable to the audience. You need to make sure that all of the content you present is going to add value to the lives of the audience in some

way. If you have a lot of fluff, just throw that out because it will make the audience bored and they will not take you seriously.

➤ Humor—people will always remember a speaker who was able to make them laugh. The earlier that you are able to get the audience smiling and laughing with you the more memorable your speech is going to be. This is because it is going to help make the audience around you more receptive to the ideas that you are getting across. Having humor in your speech does not mean that you must be a comedian, just add in a few jokes and some irony and you are sure to get the audience on your side.

➤ Organization—before going out for a speech, you must make sure that you are completely organized. Have all of the facts checked, the information in order, and everything in its place. There is no excuse that allows you to ramble on through the presentation. This is just going to make the audience get lost or make you lose your credibility. If you are organized, you are leaving your audience with a message that they can understand and which is easy to remember.

➤ Approachable—the best speakers are the ones who seem like they are approachable. These are the ones who will meet and greet people before and after the speech and who will leave room for questions at some point. These are the speakers who do not seem like they are in a rush to leave right away but instead would rather spend their time with the audience.

➤ Authentic—people want to know who you really are; they are smart enough to know when you are trying to pull one over on them and they will become less receptive if they feel like you are doing this. They want to hear someone who is going to be honest to them. If you are a shy person, it is fine to show this out a little in the speech because it lets people know that even though this is your fear, you feel that your message is important enough to share.

➢ Natural—when you are up in front of an audience, you should try to act natural and calm. This will help the audience to feel like there is a connection and they will be able to listen more closely this way. It can often spell disaster if you are sitting there acting off or being too nervous. Try to act like the audience is some of your close friends and you are sharing something with them rather than worrying about a large crowd.

➢ Passion—a good speaker is someone who is really passionate about what they are saying. They know that their information is valuable and useful and they want to get it out to the audience. When you are excited about the message, the audience is going to catch on to that excitement and they will be excited soon as well.

Chapter 2:
Look the Part

Now that you know about some of the characteristics that you should look out for when getting ready for your next speech, it is time to learn how to look the part. Think about all of the public speaking events that you have been to in the past; what was the speaker wearing? Would a different outfit made you listen or pay attention to the speaker in a different way than you did. The way that you dress is just as important as the things that you say to the audience. Without the right outfit, no one is going to take you seriously and you will just be wasting your time.

It is never a good idea to go to a speech wearing jeans that have a lot of holes in them, a tank top, and some flip flops. This is something that would get you attention at the beach, but will probably get you in trouble with your speaking engagement. If you want to come across in a way that projects confidence and that you are a credible speaker when you are making a presentation, you need to make sure that you are dressing for the right success. In fact, there has been research done that states how 93 percent of your impact from communication is going to come from the way that you sound and the way that you look. This section is going to help you learn how to ditch those jeans and instead pick something that will work so much better for public appearance.

The first thing that you need to consider is how you are looking to the audience. Is the outfit that you wearing give you the credibility that you want, command attention and imbue you with power? Or is our outfit something that is uncertain, sloppy, and week. Would your outfit be something that is distracting from your message or is it helping you to look professional? It is important to get these questions down right away if you would like to see the right results to go with your speech.

Looking Good

Today, there are many different ways that you will be able to look good for a speech and they do not all require the traditional suit and tie like they did in the past. This does not mean that you are not able to wear a suit and a tie if you feel comfortable in these or if you feel that the message of the speech could be delivered in a better way if you were wearing this outfit. It simply means that you have a little bit more freedom to choose your speaking outfit than what was present in the past so if you are not comfortable in a suit and tie, you can make other options. Just make sure that you are always looking your best when you get up in front of the audience because there are going to be many sets of eyes that are focused on you. It is a good idea to make sure that any outfit you choose is not too snug or that you keep an extra pair of panty hose in case they get a run so that you can switch out if something happens. Make sure that all of your garments are well-fitting and clean pressed.

Another thing to keep in mind is that you should not choose an outfit based just on how good it looks, although this is important. You should also make sure to pick out an outfit that makes you feel good as well. If you are uncomfortable in an outfit, which is going to show through in the speech and can make the audience uncomfortable as well. Pick out something that looks nice and makes you feel great so that you are able to leave with some confidence.

Fabric Choice

When picking out your outfit, you should choose fabrics that are going to keep you cool and which will not show your sweat. It can get really hot when you are nervous about something so it is not a good idea to pick out fabrics that are heavy and will not breathe. You should not choose man made fabrics such as polyester since these are not going to breathe very well for you. Natural fabrics such as silk, wool, and cotton all look nice and can breathe just the way that you need them to.

Being appropriate

It does not matter how nice you think you look in an outfit, if it is not appropriate than you should not put it on for the function. You need to consider what is appropriate both for the occasion as well as for the audience at hand. Depending on the context for the speech, a floor length ball gown can be just as inappropriate as a bathing suit. What will work to wear in front of a board of directors will not always work when you are talking to a group of construction workers who are wearing flannel shirts and jeans.

One thing that you can do is wear something that is business casual and throw a jacket over. The jacket will give it more of the elegance that you will need so that you can fit into a suit and tie situation if needed, but if you find that the event is more laid back, you can take off the coat and still fit in. Another rule to remember is that the more skin that is exposed the more casual your look is. This means that a no-sleeves top will serve this principle better than short sleeves and a lot better than long sleeves. This is the same for any outfit that you might choose to wear. You can keep this in mind when determining what kind of outfit you should wear for your event.

Color

The colors that you are wearing are just as important as anything else and your audience will be taking in the color of the outfit that you are wearing as they are listening to you. Black and navy are often considered power colors, but the issue comes when most people do not look that great in them. If you do not look good in a color, it can be really distracting to the message that you are trying to get across. It is best to choose a color that compliments your eye color, hair, and skin color. Most people will be either in cool tones or in warm tones and over time you will be better able to tell which one is going to work the best for you. If you make the wrong color choices, you will either be washed out by the colors of your outfit or you are going to clash with the coloring, both of which will not work as appearance enhancers before the crowd.

One other thing that you should remember is what occurs when you wear two contrasting colors, such as black pants and a white shirt; you are basically using the colors in order to split your body into two. This is going to create an illusion of a wider and shorter figure. Most people do not like this idea and so would rather find a way to make themselves look slender and taller. To do this, you should go for a monochrome look, one that has the top matching with the bottom.

The choices that you make in clothes will make all the difference in how you feel and present your speech. If you feel good in the clothes that you are wearing, you will be able to portray that out to the audience better. It is a good idea to check ahead of your event so that you are able to determine an outfit that will go with the occasion as well as one that makes you look and feel good.

Chapter 3:
How to Practice Public Speaking

One of the best things that you can do in order to get over any nervousness that you have and to prepare of your public speaking is to practice. This might seem like something that you should not have to do; you have all of the information right in front of you and you have been spending a lot of time on the project so you feel like you are an expert on anything that has to do with this topic. While that might be true, it can be a completely different experience when you get up and actually begin talking about the subject. You might find that your notes are not enough; that you are not sure how to do transitions; that you freeze up; or that your flow is not as smooth or you need to add something else in. It is much better to find out about these things before you get up in front of a lot of people and make the mistakes. Practice at least a few times before you have to go up in front of the audience and talk to them, but if you have time to do it many times, then you should do that as well. This chapter discusses some of the tips that you should take in order to effectively practice your public speaking.

Write out your speech

One of the things that you might like trying out is to write out your speech. Get out some paper and a pen or use a computer if you think that will be easier. The writing tools do not matter as much as getting something that will be able to capture everything that you plan on saying during the speech. You should write out the introduction, then the middle, and finally the end, trying to stay as close to word for word as you are able to. Of course, when you get up and talk in front of people, you are going to change around some of the wording or say something that is a little bit different, but at least now you will have something that is written down that you will be able to practice from. You should also read through what you have written in order to find out if there are any spots that are really awkward or if there seems to be any information that is missing.

Memorize Your Speech

This one might seem like it is a little bit out there, but you should use the speech that you just wrote out and learn it all by heart. You should read off the sheet a few times to start so that you can get the pacing and the tone of voice down without having to remember all of the words. After a few times, you will feel a little more confident about what is going on and you will eventually not need to have the paper anymore. When you are practicing, find somewhere in your home or in your office that is secluded and where you will be able to be alone. This is a great way to build up the confidence that you need to give your speech and sound amazing while you are doing it.

When doing this step, you need to learn how to be natural when talking. Even though you have memorized the speech, you do not want to sound like you are just reading off the screen. Instead, pretend that you are an actor and this is your script. You need to add in some passion, something extra to get the audience's attention and make them feel like you really know what you are talking about. If you just read from memorization, the audience is going to notice and they are going to get bored really easily. The point of memorizing your speech is to give you the confidence that is needed to keep going and to not falter. You will then be able to go off the script a little bit if you need and then go back if you begin to fumble. This is a great way to give yourself a little bit of freedom during the whole process.

Practice Speech Out Loud

It is important that you take the time to practice your speech out loud once you have it memorized. You should start from the beginning and work all the way through the body of the speech before ending with the conclusion. It is best to try and do it the same way that you would in front of the audience; if you are skipping around or just practicing one part and not the other, you might find that you are not as prepared as you would like when it comes time to talk to the audience. Also, while you are talking out loud, pretend that there are others in the room with you, even though there is not going to be anyone there. You should not only practice the words that you are going to say, but practice the inflections that will go with the words, the hand gestures, your movements, and any comedy that you plan to throw into the mix. The more that you practice all of this and put thought into it, the better it is going to come out when you are all done.

The important part about this step is that you practice as closely as you can to how you would like the speech to come out when you actually meet the audience. Everything that you practice is going to seem much more natural if you do it at least a few times before. If you spend all of your time just learning the words and nothing else, you are going to sound really stilted and hard to understand when it comes time to give the speech.

Practice without the Notes

It is important to start the presentation practice with the notes on hand. This will allow you to go through everything while just looking down if you forget something rather than going through things later and finding out that you were completely wrong. After you have had some time to practice with your notes, it is time to drop them and practice without. Ideally, you are going to have enough time before the presentation that you can learn the material and not have to keep notecards or other papers around with you. Of course, if you are only given a few days to put the whole thing together you might not have time to do this, but if you have a month or more to prepare, it is going to look more natural on stage if you are able to give your speech without any of the notes at all.

You can start this part off slowly, perhaps do each section of your speech without the notes a few times so you can get it down. After a couple of runs, you will realize that you already know the material and you do not need to have it on you in order to be successful.

Record Yourself

Once you begin to feel comfortable with your speech and everything that you are saying, it is a good idea to record yourself. First, get out a little radio recorder and have it turned on while you are saying the speech. Go through the whole speech without stopping or worrying about what you are doing. When you are done with the speech, sit down with a pen and paper and then listen to the audio recording from the beginning to the end. Do not worry too much about how the speech sounds and instead use this as a learning experience. Take down notes of what you have done wrong, spending more time on the delivery of the speech rather than if you missed some information or not. If you have a lot of ummms in your speech, figure out how you can get rid of these so that the whole thing flows together better. You will also be able to catch on to things that you thought were good to have in the speech, but now that you are hearing them played back they sound really bad or really forced. Make adjustments to your speech and then do it again with the recorder. You will find that each time you do this process, you are going to get more comfortable with the recorder and things will begin to fall into place. Continue doing this process until you think that everything sounds perfect.

After you have gotten everything to sound good on the audio recording, it is time to bring out a camcorder and do it over again. Take a video of yourself giving the speech, following the same steps as before. The point of this process is that you will now be able to see how you look to the audience. Are you twitching a lot or wringing your hands in nervousness? Do you look like you are about to fall over? You should also make sure that you are wearing the outfit that you will have on at the speech so you can see how you look with that and with your speech. Do this a couple of times until you get everything down.

These steps should be able to prepare you to give your speech in a natural way to the audience. You will have had plenty of practice with your speech and can almost recite in in your dreams. This can help you to continue on during the process without the hindrance of your notes or having to worry about forgetting important information. It can also help you to get the confidence that you need to keep on going, even if you make a mistake, and that confidence is going to radiate out to the audience and make them like you and your ideas.

Chapter 4:
Tips for Public Speaking

Here are some tips that you can take into account when you are getting ready to speak in front of an audience.

Getting Ready

➢ Breathe—there is nothing wrong with slowing down and taking a breath during the speech. A pause that seems really long to you is usually only a few seconds, so just breathe collect yourself and keep going when needed. It is easy to forget to breathe during the speech which can make you go through the information too fast and makes you feel really nervous. No one is going to mind if you take just a few seconds and segue to the next point in your speech; it can help to keep the pacing.

➢ Make an outline—this outline can be a lifesaver if you do not have much time to prepare and are worried about getting all of the information right. Make the font a little bit bigger so that you are able to read it with a glance rather than having to concentrate too hard and lose your space.

➢ Own your speech—you are the expert on this topic so let others know that. They have come to you for advice; do not let your anxiety get to you. You are the expert and know what you are talking about so let that get out to the audience when you are talking to them.

While Speaking

➤ Eye contact—it is a good idea to maintain eye contact with the audience while you are talking. You should be able to get your energy from the audience and they are going to be able to help you a lot more if you are able to give back to them. Look your audience in the eye while you are talking to keep them focused and to help yourself look like you are in control.

➤ Practice to avoid nervousness—one of the best things that you will be able to do if you are nervous is to go over your speech ahead of time. You will be able to learn the material better, have something to fall back on if you forget, and will gain the confidence that you need to keep on going.

➤ Save questions for the end—some speakers will feel like they should have questions open at any time. They feel this will make them more approachable to the audience. This is usually a bad idea because it is going to make your ideas get jumbled and you will lose your spot. Kindly tell the audience that you will be happy to answer their questions at the end of the speech so you can effortlessly get through the material.

Avoiding Bumps

➤ Do not panic about the timing—when you are presenting at home, you may find that you are more calm and collected. This could result in a conflict of timing if you get nervous at the presentation and talk faster. A good way to keep track of your timing so you are not trying to rush through everything is to place your watch on the podium in front of you. Then you can see exactly how much time is left and plan accordingly.

➤ Watch for nervous habits—this can include things like playing with your necklace or twirling your hair. The audience will spend more time paying attention to this rather than to your speech so learn how to avoid it or do not wear any clothing or jewelry that would present the temptation.

➤ Bring supplies—if you are worried about getting thirsty during the speech, bring along a bottle of water. This can help avoid issues with dry mouth as well as can help you if you get stuck-no one will notice a long pause if you are taking a drink from your water. Also, some tissues in your pocket are nice if you have to sneeze or have a runny nose. Bring along a few little things that you will be able to stuff in your pockets and use if the need arises.

Conclusion

Public speaking is something that anyone is able to do with a little bit of practice, knowing the material, and the right mind set. You do not have to go into a speech feeling nervous and like you are not in control. With the help of this guidebook, you will be able to grab the control that you want and get the audience to listen to you during your speech.

Thank you again for downloading this book!

Finally, if you enjoyed this book, then I'd like to ask you for a favor, would you be kind enough to leave a review for this book on Amazon? It'd be greatly appreciated!